the ETC program

English in Everyday Life

A Competency-Based Grammar

Elaine Kirn
West Los Angeles College

Angelica Sanchez

RANDOM HOUSE New York

First Edition

9   8   7   6   5   4   3

Library of Congress Cataloging-in-Publication Data

Kirn, Elaine.
    The *ETC* program. English in everyday life: a competency-based
grammar / Elaine Kirn.
        p.   cm.
    Level 2.
    1. English language—Textbooks for foreign speakers.
2. English language—Grammar—1950-   I. Title.
PE1128.K478   1988   428.2′4—dc19
ISBN 0-394-35340-4

Manufactured in the United States of America

Series design and production: Etcetera Graphics
                    Canoga Park, California
Cover design: Juan Vargas, Vargas/Williams Design
Illustrations: Etcetera Graphics
Artist: Terry Wilson
Photo research: Marian Hartsough
Photos: Sally Gati
Typesetting: Etcetera Graphics

Contents

iii

Preface

Language is me.
Language is you.
Language is people.
Language is what people do.
Language is loving and hurting.
Language is clothes, faces, gestures, responses.
Language is imagining, designing, creating, destroying.
Language is control and persuasion.
Language is communication.
Language is laughter.
Language is growth.
Language is me.
The limits of my language are the limits of my world.

And you can't package *that* up in a book, can you?

—New Zealand Curriculum Development

No, you can't package language in a book or even a whole program of books, but you have to start somewhere.

About the *ETC* Program

ETC is a six-level ESL (English as a second language) program for adults who are learning English to improve their lives and work skills. The material of this level is divided into three books, carefully coordinated, chapter by chapter, in theme, competency goals, grammar, and vocabulary. For a visual representation of the scope and sequence of the program, see the back cover of any volume.

ETC has been designed for maximum efficiency and flexibility. To choose the materials most suitable for your particular teaching situation, decide on the appropriate level by assessing the ability and needs of the students you expect to be teaching. The competency descriptions included in each instructor's manual ("About This Level") will aid you in your assessment.

About This Book

In a structure-based ESL course, *ETC English in Everyday Life: A Competency Based Grammar* will provide the core material. Organized around grammar principles and patterns, it provides vital competency material in its reading matter, exercises, and practical activities. On the other hand, in a program that emphasizes language skills while deemphasizing structure, the grammar will serve as a supplementary workbook for the corresponding reading/writing and listening/speaking texts.

Organization

Like most other books in the *ETC* program, the grammar book of English in Everyday Life consists of an introduction and ten chapters, each divided into four parts with specific purposes.

• *Parts One, Two and Three* begin with a strip story or conversation that introduces the important vocabulary and the grammar of that section; these three parts present and practice sentence structures central to the language, such as verb tenses.

• *Part Four* begins with specific grammar points, such as the use of prepositions, kinds of nouns, and quantity expressions; it then summarizes and reviews the previous material of the chapter.

Symbols

The following symbols appear throughout the text:

✳ a challenging activity designed for more advanced students

Available Ancillaries

The instructor's annotated edition for this text includes:

- a general introduction to the *ETC* program, this level, and this book
- general suggestions for teaching techniques to use in presenting the various kinds of activities
- page-by-page teacher's notes next to the reduced pages of the student text to which they refer
- an answer key provided on the reduced text pages
- progress tests, one to accompany each chapter of the text, that can be duplicated and distributed to students
- an answer key for the progress tests

Acknowledgments

To Etcetera, ETC, ETC, because we finally did it.

Appreciation beyond frustration goes to the many class testers and reviewers, reviewers, reviewers—whose opinions lie at the core of the *ETC* Program. Thanks to the following reviewers, whose comments both favorable and critical, were of great value in the development of *ETC English in Everyday Life*:

Peter T. Bomba, Carol Cargill-Vroman, Nancy Frothingham, Alice Gosak, Julia Jolly, Nick Kremer, Carolyn McCarthy, Maryann O'Brien, Nancy Olds, Kara Rosenberg, Edward Schiffer, Margaret Segal, Jane Sturtevant, Kent Sutherland, Elizabeth Templin, Mary Thurber, Jane Turner, Stephanie Vandrick, Julia Villasenor, Betsey Warrick, Patricia K. Werner, Roni R. Wong, Synthia Woodcock.

The author wishes to thank the staff at Random House:
- Eirik Borve and Karen Judd—for keeping promises,
- Lesley Walsh—for being as efficient as ever,
- Marian Hartsough—for communicating where need be, and
- Edith Brady, Cynthia Ward, and the sales staff—for what is yet to come.

Heartfelt thanks to the staff and supporters of Etcetera Graphics, Canoga Park, California:
- Susan Smith Amatori—for copyediting and typemarking,
- Terry Wilson—for his inspired artwork and patience,
- Cindra Tardif—for expert typesetting, and
- Sheila Clark—for alert and patient production,

and gratitude, appreciation, and love to
- Anthony Thorne-Booth—for his management, expertise, and hard work,
- Karol Roff—for helping, helping, helping,
- Sally Kostal—for jumping in to rescue us and to keep us calm,
- Chuck Alessio—for everything and more

and to Andi Kirn—for putting up with it all.

E.K.

Introduction

Starting Out

COMPETENCIES:
Introducing oneself and others
Asking about vocabulary and naming things

GRAMMAR REVIEW:
Subject pronouns and possessive adjectives
Contractions with *be*
Singular and plural: *this/that/these/those*

1

What's your name?	Helga
How do you spell it?	H-e-l-g-a
Where are you from?	Switzerland

A. Finish the questions with these words. (Say or write them.) Answer them.

| do | What's | from | are |

1. **What's** your name?   My name is Angélica

2. How **do** you spell it?   A-N-G-É-L-I-C-A

3. Where **are** you **from** ?   I'm from Zacatecas

| My
Your
His
Her | name is _Angélica_ . | I'm
You're
He's
She's | from _Zacatecas_ |
| I'm = I am   you're = you are   he's = he is   she's = she is |

B. Finish these sentences. (Play a name game.)

My name is _Eloy_
I'm from _Zacatecas_

Your name is _Araceli_
You're from _Zacatecas_
My name is _María_
I'm from _Guadalajara_

[His / Her] name is _____
[He's / She's] from _____
Your name is _____
You're from _____
My name is _____
I'm from _____

*C. Make sentences about you and your classmates and teacher. (Say or write them.)

EXAMPLES: a: His name is Ja-Ja Nkrumah. He's from Nigeria.
b: My teacher is Mr. Bright. He's from Canada.

Singular	What's this in English? What's that?	It's a list. It's paper.
	what's = what is	it's = it is
Plural	What are these? What are those?	They're pencils. They're lights.
		they're = they are

D. Ask and answer questions about the things in this picture with these words and words of your own.

EXAMPLES: a: What's that in English?
b: It's the **chalkboard**.

Singular				Plural			
the door	a desk	a list	chalk	windows	tables	pencils	erasers
the chalkboard	a clock	a map	paper	lights	chairs	pens	cards

*E. Say or write sentences about things in your classroom. Ask and answer questions.

EXAMPLES: a: What are those in English?
b: They're shelves. And those are magazines.

CHAPTER

1

Getting There

COMPETENCIES:
Giving and following instructions and directions
Telling rules
Expressing ability and permission
Asking for directions
Making requests

GRAMMAR:
The imperative
Can/can't
Pronouns
Prepositions

PART ONE / The Imperative: Affirmative and Negative

● Giving and Following Instructions and Directions

Take the bus to school.

Get your books.
Leave the house . . .

Don't drive the car.
Take the bus.

You're late. Don't walk.
Run to the bus stop.

Wait for the bus.
But don't sit on the bench.

Get on the bus.
Don't forget your books.

Don't read the newspaper.
Watch the signs.

Get off at Grand Avenue.
Then cross the street.

Go into the school.
Look for your classroom.

Welcome to the class!

| Leave | the house. | Go | into | the school. |
| Watch | the signs. | Look | for | your classroom. |

A. Make sentences with these words. (Say or write them.)

EXAMPLES: 1. Get your books.
2. Leave the house.

1. Get ———————— the house.

2. Leave ———————— your books.

3. Run ———————— for the bus.

4. Wait ———————— to the bus stop.

5. Get on ———————— the school.

6. Read ———————— the street.

7. Cross ———————— the bus.

8. Walk into ———————— the signs.

B. Finish the sentences with these words.

EXAMPLE: 1. **Sit** on the bench.

| Take | Read | Watch | Sit | Look | Walk |

1. _Sit_ on the bench.

2. _Watch_ the newspaper.

3. _Take_ the bus.

4. _Read_ the signs.

5. _Walk_ into the school.

6. _Loon_ for your classroom.

| Don't turn left. | don't = do not |
| Don't read the newspaper. | |

C. Finish the sentences with these words.

| Don't park cross drive sit make turn |

1. _Don't Park_ here.
2. _Don't sit_ on the bench.
3. _Don't cross_ the street now.

4. _Don't drive_ in here.
5. _Don't turn_ left.
6. _Don't make_ a U-turn.

| Don't Park park Turn turn Sit sit |

 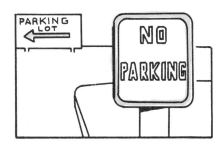 

7. _Don't turn_ right.
8. _Turn_ left.

9. _Don't park_ on the street.
10. _Park_ in the lot.

11. _Don't sit_ on the grass.
12. _Sit_ on the bench.

*D. Give instructions from your school to your house or apartment. You can use the pictures for ideas, but add information of your own, too.

EXAMPLES: 1. Get your books. Leave the classroom.
2. Go out of the school. Walk to the parking lot.
3. Get in the car. Drive to Central Avenue.
4. Park on the street. Get out of the car.
5. Go into the apartment building. Open the door.
6. Put your books on the table. Sit down.

**E. Give and follow classroom instructions.

EXAMPLES: 1. Go to the chalkboard. Write your name.
2. Get your book. Open it to page 10.
3. Take a pencil. Write the answers on paper.
4. Give the teacher your paper.

PART TWO / *Can/Can't*; Pronouns

● Telling Rules   ● Expressing Ability and Permission

You can't park here.

You	can't	park	here.
We	can	go	to the parking lot.

can't = cannot

A. Make sentences with these words. (Say or write them.)

EXAMPLE: 1. Don't turn left.

1. _Don't turn left_
   left / turn / Don't / .

2. _Don't park here_
   park / here / Don't / .

3. _You can't park on the street_
   on the street / can't / You / park / .

4. _You can drive to the lot_
   can / drive / to the lot / You / .

B. Finish the sentences with these words.

don't	can	can't

EXAMPLE: 1. We **can't** sit on the grass.

We _can't_ sit on the grass. But we _can_ sit on this bench. We _don't_ eat
   1.   **2.**   **3.**

lunch in the classroom. But _don't_ worry. We _can_ eat here. And please _can't_
                                4.   **5.**   **6.**

study now.

Please _can_ speak quickly to my father. He _don't_ understand English well. But
       7.   **8.**

my mother _can_ .
         9.

I   we   you   you

it   he   she   they

C. Make sentences for the picture with these words and words of your own.

EXAMPLES: **a:** I can wait for the bus here.
b: He can't park in the lot.

| I We You He She They | can can't | park in the lot. go into the school. speak English well. enroll in English classes. wait for the bus here. _____ |

_____***D.**   **Choose words and finish these sentences. You can get ideas from the pictures, but add information of your own, too.**

EXAMPLES: 1. I can **read English well**.
            2. We can't **eat lunch in this room**.
            3. The teacher can't **take the bus to school**.

I			I		
We			We		
The teacher	can	_write_ .	You	can't	_speak English_
He			My classmates		
She			They		

_____****E.**   **Tell or write about your school. Use *can* or *can't*. (You can work in small groups.)**

EXAMPLES: a: We **can** enroll in classes at any time.
            b: You **can** take one English class. You **can't** take two.
            c: Teachers **can** park in the lot, but students **can't**.

PART THREE

Can/Can't; *Yes/No* Questions and Answers

● Asking for Directions

Can you give us directions, please?

me	us	you	him	her	it	them

A. Choose the correct words. (Say or circle them.)

Can [**I** / me] get some information? How about your mother? Can [she / **her**]
1.   2.

understand English well? And your father? Can [**he** / him] understand [**it** / its] ? Here
3.   4.

are enrollment cards for [he / **him**] and [she / **her**] . Please take [they / **them**] .
5.   6.   7.

B. Finish the sentences with these words. (Say or write them.)

me	I	you	they	them

Excuse _me_ . Can _you_ please give _me_ directions to the office?
1.   2.   3.

No, sorry, _I_ can't. Why don't _you_ ask _them_ ? Maybe _they_ can.
4.   5.   6.   7.

we	us	you	he	him

Sorry, _we_ can't help _you_ . Why don't _you_ talk to _____ ? Maybe
8.   9.   10.   11.

_____ can give _____ directions. And then please tell _____ .
12.   13.   14.

you	she	her	it

Sorry. But go to _____ . Maybe _____ can give _____ a map. Take _____
15.   16.   17.   18.

and read _____ .
19.

Can	you	give	me directions, please?	Yes,	I	can.
Can	we	get	some information?	No,	we	can't.
Can	they	speak	English well?		you	
					they	

C. Have conversations with these words.

EXAMPLES: 1. a: Can I park here?
            b: Yes, you can.

1.

a: _Can I park here_
    park here / Can / I / ?

b: _Yes, you can_
    you / Yes, / can / .

2.

a: _Can you watch them ?_
    you / watch them / Can / ?

b: Sorry. _No, I can't_
        can't / I / No, / .

3.

a: _Can we eat here_
    eat here / Can / we / ?

b: _No you can't_ Sorry.
    you / No, / can't / .

4.

a: _Can they come to the office?_
    they / come to the office / Can / ?

b: Of course _They can_
         can / they / .

**D. Choose words and finish this question. Answer it.

EXAMPLES: a. Can you write **English well**?   b. Yes, I can.
           a. Can the teacher **speak Chinese**?   b. No, she can't.
           a. Can we **buy books at this school**?   b. Yes, we can.

| Can | we
you
the teacher
he / she
your classmates
they | _____ ? |

PART FOUR / Prepositions; Review

● Making Requests

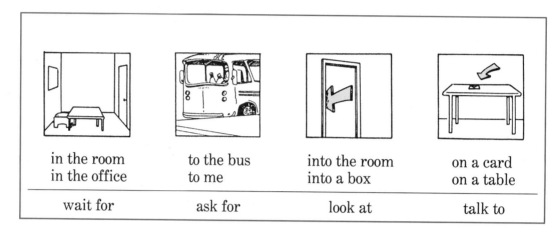

in the room in the office	to the bus to me	into the room into a box	on a card on a table
wait for	ask for	look at	talk to

A. Choose the correct words. (Say or circle them.)

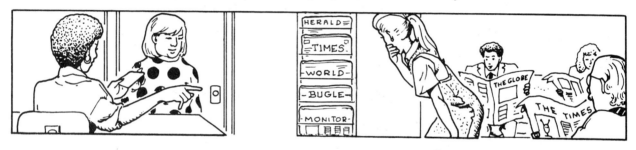

Please write your name [in /(on)] the card. Then give it [(to)/ at] me. Can you wait
          1.   **2.**

[to /(for)] your friends here [(in)/ into] the office? You can look [(at)/ to] those
3.   **4.**   **5.**

newspapers. And you can talk [at /(to)] those students.
                         6.

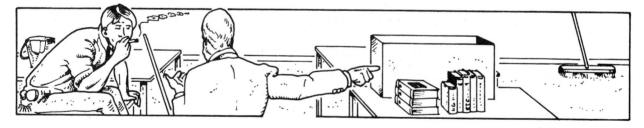

Please don't smoke [(in)/ on] the classroom. And don't sit [in /(on)] the table. Please
                 7.   **8.**

put those books [for /(into)] the box. Can you take the box [with /(to)] the office?
           9.   **10.**

		Look	at	the pictures.
	Don't	take		the car.
We	can	wait	on	the bench.
You	can't	make		a U-turn here.
Can	I	read		your newspaper, please?

B. Make sentences with these words.

EXAMPLE:
1. Please **take an enrollment card**.
   Then **write the information**.
   You can **use this pencil**.
   But don't **keep it**.

Please _put these car in the box_
Then _take the box to the office_
You can _sit on the .char_
But don't _sit on the .box._

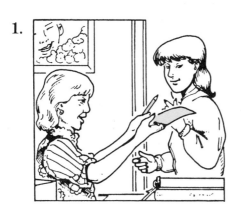

1.
take an enrollment card
write the information
use this pencil
keep it

2.
put these cards in the box
take the box to the office
sit on a chair
sit on the box

3
get your books
open them to page 16
read the instructions
write the answers now

4.
give me your papers
go to lunch
sit on the grass
eat in the classroom

C. Have conversations with these words.

EXAMPLE:

1. a: Can I help you?
   b: Yes, please. Can I **enroll in a class**?
   a: Of course you can. But I'm sorry. You can't **smoke in the office**.

a: Can I help you?
b: Yes, please. Can I _____ ?
a: Of course you can. But I'm sorry. You can't _____ .

1.
b: enroll in a class
a: smoke in the office

2.
b: look at this map
a: take it with you

3.
b: park in the lot
a: turn left here

EXAMPLE:

4. a: Can you **speak English well**?
   b: No, sorry, I can't. But I can **read and write it**.
   a: You can? Then please **help me with this card**.

a: Can you _____ ?
b: No, sorry, I can't. But I can _____ .
a: You can? Then please _____ .

4.
a: speak English well
b: read and write it
a: help me with this card

5.
a: make a U-turn here
b: go left
a: turn at Elm Street

6.
a: drive me to school
b: give you directions to the bus stop
a: draw a map for me

*D Choose words and have conversations of your own.

1. a: Excuse me, please. Can you _____ ?
   b: [Yes, / No,] I [can / can't] .

2. a: Can I please _____ ?
   b: [Yes, of course. / No, sorry] .

3. a: Please _____ . And don't _____ .
   b: All right.

4. a: I can _____ , but I can't _____ .
   b: Really? Well, I can't _____ , but I can _____ .

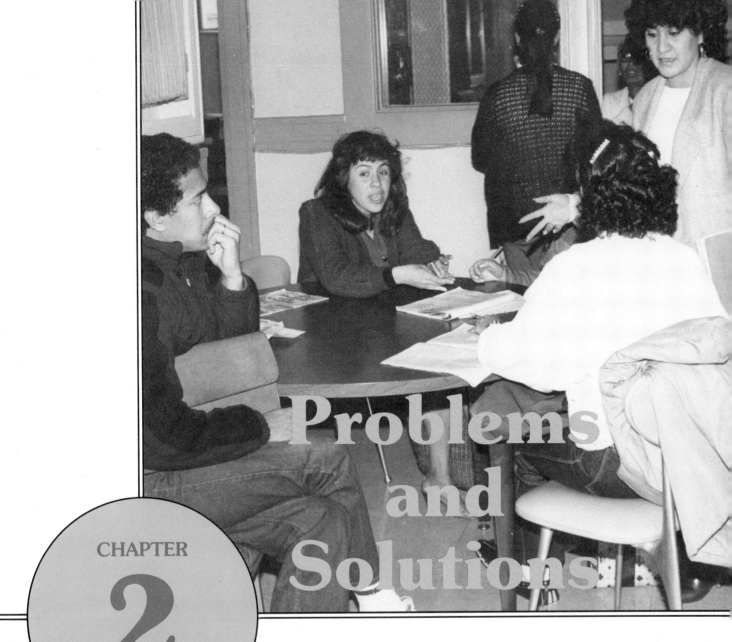

Problems and Solutions

CHAPTER 2

COMPETENCIES:
Describing situations
Asking about problems
Suggesting solutions to problems
Telling places and times

GRAMMAR:
The simple present
Prepositions
Kinds of nouns

PART ONE   The Simple Present: Affirmative and Negative Statements

● Telling about Problems

I have a problem.

> I   want   a new car.
> We   need   new furniture.

A.   Finish the sentences with these words. (Say or write them.)

EXAMPLE: **1.** We **need** more room in our apartment.

need	have	make	talk	work	smoke	want

We ___need___ more room in our apartment. We
1.

___have___ four children.
2.

I ___want___ more money. But I ___work___ at
3.   **4.**

two jobs now.

My roommates ___make___ noise. They ___talk___
5.   **6.**

on the telephone from morning to night. They

___smoke___ cigarettes.
7.

> They   don't   clean   the house. | don't = do not

B.   Finish the sentences with these words.

don't	can't

We ___don't___ like our apartment. But we ___can't___ pay the rent for a big
1.   **2.**

house. And managers ___don't___ want children in apartments, you know. They
3.

___don't___ understand our problem. We ___can't___ find another place.
4.   **5.**

have	read	write	understand

People don't ___understand___ my English. I can't ___write___ letters. I can't
                      6.   **7.**

___read___ English newspapers. I need more classes. But I don't ___have___ time.
8.   **9.**

C. Make new sentences with the underlined words.

EXAMPLE: 1. a: **They can't speak** English.
                b: **They can't speak** Japanese.

**Our friends
come over on
Saturdays.**

**My friends
come over on
Saturdays, too.**

1. **They can't speak** English.   _They can't speak_ Japanese.

2. **We have** parties.   _We have_ quiet conversations.

3. We **don't like** a quiet place.   I _don't like_ a noisy place.

4. We **can't stand** a clean
   apartment.   I _can't stand_ a dirty
                                         apartment.

D.   Make sentences with the opposite meaning.

EXAMPLE: 1. a: We **don't like** American food.
                b: I **like** American food.

1. We **don't like** American food.   I _I like American food_

2. We **can't cook**.   I _can cook_

3. We **don't watch** T.V.   I _watch T.V._

4. We **play** music.   I _don't play music_

5. We **smoke**.   I _don't smoke_

*E.   Choose words and finish the sentences about you. You can use the pictures for ideas, but add information of your own, too. (You can work in small groups.)

EXAMPLES: a: I want **a big T.V. and a stereo set**.
                b: I don't like **television**, but I like **music**.

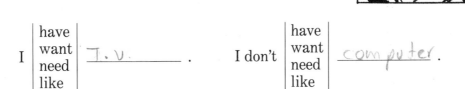

I | have
  | want   _T.V._   .
  | need
  | like

I don't | have
        | want   _computer_ .
        | need
        | like

**F.   From the information above, choose a roommate for you. Tell or write your reasons.

EXAMPLE: Anna and I can be roommates because she can cook, and I like food.

PART TWO   The Simple Present: *Yes/No* Questions and Answers

● Asking about Problems

Do you study?

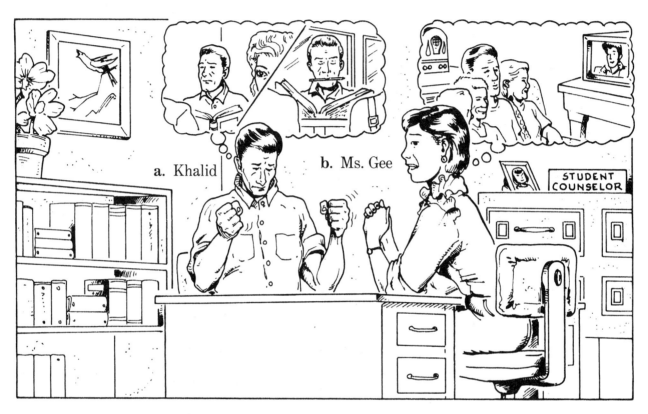

a. Khalid   b. Ms. Gee

a: I can't learn English. I try. But I can't.

b: You can't? Why not?

a: Excuse me? I don't understand.

b: Can you see in class? Can you hear?

a: Yes, I can.

b: Hmmm . . . well, do your teachers help you?

a: Yes, they do.

b: Do you study?

a: Yes, I do. I study on the bus. You see, I don't have time at home.

b: Oh. And do you come to class all week?

a: No, I don't. I work all day, and I'm too tired.

b: I see. Well, do the people in your family use English?

a: No, they don't.

b: Do you and your family watch T.V. a lot? Do you listen to the radio?

a: Yes, we do. We like the music. But we don't listen to the people. They speak English.

b: Hmmm . . . I understand your problem.

Do	you	watch	T.V.?	Yes,	we do.
Do	they	help	you?	No,	they don't.

A. Finish the questions and answers with these words. (Say or write them.)

Can	can	Do	do	don't

1. _Can_ you see in class? Yes, I _can_.

2. _Do_ your teachers help you? Yes, they _do_.

3. _Do_ you study? Yes, I _do_.

4. And _do_ you come to class all week? No, I _don't_.

*Now answer the above questions with information about you.

B. Have conversations with these words.

EXAMPLE: **1.** **a:** Do you **study English every day**?
b: No, I don't.
But I **come to school all week**.
a: Can you **take more classes**?
b: **No, I can't.**

a: Do you _have a job_?
b: No, I don't.
But I _need money_
a: Can you _use a computer_?
b: No, I can't.

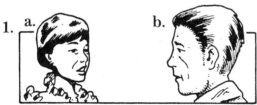

1.

a: study English every day
b: come to school all week
a: take more classes

2. JOB BOARD

a: have a job
b: need money
a: use a computer

3. HOUSES AND APARTMENTS

a: live in a big apartment
b: need more room
a: pay the rent for it

4.

a: _Do you live in a big apartment?_
b: _No, I don't. But I need more room?_
a: _Can you pay the rent for it?_

_____ **C.** **Ask questions for these answers.**

EXAMPLE: **a:** Can you see and hear in class?
b: Yes, I can. I can see and hear in class very well.

1. _Can you see and hear in class very well_ ?
Yes, I can. I can see and hear in class very well.

2. _Do your teachers help you_ ?
Yes, they do. My teachers help me all the time.

3. _Do you study_ ?
Yes, I do. I study on the weekends.

4. _Do you come to class every day_ ?
No, I don't. I can't come to class every day.

5. _Can your family understand English_ ?
No, they can't. The people in my family can't understand English.

*Now answer the above questions with information about you.

_____ ***D.** **Make questions from these words and words of your own. Answer them.**

EXAMPLE: **a:** Do you know English well?
b: Yes, I do.

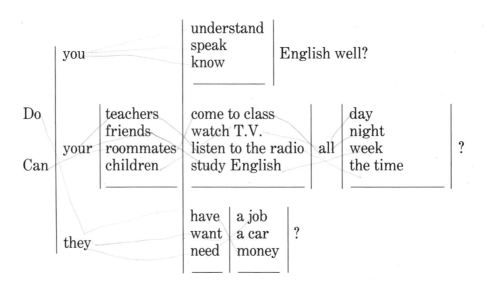

PART THREE
The Simple Present: Questions and Answers

● Suggesting Solutions to Problems

When do you practice English?

a. Ms. Gee   b. Ms. Schmidt

*a: Problems, problems, problems. All the students have problems.

b: What do you mean?

a: For example, where do they live? In small apartments.

b: Why don't they move?

a: Because they can't pay the rent for big places. And they can't make more money because they don't know English well. But what do they speak with their families? Their native languages.

b: When do they practice English?

a: Only during class.

b: Where do they study?

a: Only at school. Why can't they study at home? They don't have room. They live in small apartments.

b: I understand. Well, how are you today?

a: Terrible. Why can't I move from my small apartment? Because I can't pay the rent for a big place. How can I get a better job? I don't have enough skills. When can I take classes? I don't have time. What do I do all day? I work. Problems, problems, problems.

What	do	your friends	speak?	
Where	do	they	study?	
When	do	your teachers	help	you with your English?
Why	can't	you	move	from your apartment?
How	can	we	get	better jobs?

what	= things	(**Examples:** English, my native language, a job)
where	= places	(**Examples:** on the bus, in class, at home)
when	= times	(**Examples:** at 8:00 in the morning, on the weekend)
why	= reasons	(**Example:** because we don't have money)
how	= ways	(**Examples:** I take the bus. I can study more.)

A. Finish the questions with these words. (Say or write them.) Then find the answers.

EXAMPLE: **a:** Do you like your apartment?
            b: Yes, we do.

Do	do	don't	Can

1. _Do_ you like your apartment?   Because I can't drive.

2. How _do_ you get to school?   Yes, we do.

3. Why _don't_ you buy a car?   We take the bus.

4. Where _can_ your children work?   In a store.

5. Why _don't_ they like their jobs?   No, they can't.

6. _Can_ they get better jobs?   Because they want more money.

7. What _do_ you speak at home?   At school.

8. When _do_ you practice English?   Our native language.

9. Where _do_ you study?   At night.

10. How _do_ you find the time?   I don't sleep a lot.

*Now answer the above questions with information about you.

B. Read the answers. Then finish the questions with these words.

EXAMPLE: 1. a: **Where do** your friends live now?
              b: In a small apartment.

Why	When	Where	How	do

1. Where do ____ your friends live now?   In a small apartment.

2. Why do ____ they want a new apartment?   Because they need more room.

3. When do ____ they look at places?   On the weekends.

4. How do ____ they get there?   They drive.

What do you do at night? I watch T.V.	What do you do? = Do you work at night?

C. Have conversations with these words.

EXAMPLE: a: What do you do **in the morning**?   a: What do you do In the after?noon
          b: I **take English classes**.   b: I go to work

1. in the morning?
   take English classes

2. in the afternoon?
   go to work

3. in your job?
   carry boxes

4. in the evening?
   play with the children

5. at night?
   study

6. (a question and answer of your own)

*Now answer the above questions with information about you.

___D. Add words and ask questions. Answer them.

EXAMPLE:
   1. a: Where do you live?
      b: In a house with my mother.

1. _Where do you live?_
     Where / you live?

2. _Where do you work?_
     Where / you work?

3. _When do you come to school?_
     When / you come to school?

4. _How do you get here?_
     How / you get here?

5. _what do you do all day?_
     What / you do all day?

6. _Why don't you practice English more_
     Why not / you practice English more?

___*E. Choose words and finish the questions. Answer them. You can use the pictures for ideas, but add information of your own, too.

EXAMPLES:
   a: What do you **do**?
   b: I drive a bus. Where do you **work**?
   a: In an office.

What
Where | do you _____?
When
How

Why don't you _____?

PART FOUR / Prepositions; Kinds of Nouns; Review

● Telling Places and Times

Place	Time		
in an office	in the morning	look	at
at home	at 8:30	look	for
on Main Street	on Mondays	wait	for
on the bus	from morning to	talk	to
to work	night = all day	listen	to

A. Choose the correct words. (Say or circle them.)

I work hard [(from) / at] Monday [on /(to)] Friday. I get up [(at)/ in] 7:00
        1.   2.   3.

[at /(in)] the morning. I take the bus [at /(to)] work. I read the newspaper [at /(on)] the
4.   5.   6.

bus. I don't have time [at /(in)] home. I work [at /(in)] an office. I type [(from)/ of]
                        7.   8.   9.

morning [at /(to)] night. I talk [at /(on)] the phone. I listen [at /(to)] people all day.
          10.   11.   12.

[(At)/ In] 6:00 I wait [on /(for)] the bus again [at /(on)] Main Street. I can't stand this
13.   14.   15.

job. [(On)/ In] Sundays I look [on /(at)] the "Help Wanted" ads. I talk [(to)/ for]
      16.   17.   18.

friends about jobs. But I can't look [to /(for)] a new job [at /(on)] Mondays. I work
                                      19.   20.

[(from)/ at] Monday [on /(to)] Friday.
21.   22.

Singular (one)	Plural (two or more)	Noncount
a problem	problems	money
a bus	buses	food
a car	cars	rent
a radio	radios	furniture
a job	jobs	music
a party	parties	noise
a friend	friends	room
a child	children	
a roommate	roommates	
a house	houses	
an apartment	apartments	
an office	offices	

B. Finish the sentences with *a*, *an*, or no word.

EXAMPLES: 1. I can't stand buses.
           2. I want **a** car.

Problems, problems, problems. I can't stand _____ busses. I want ___a___ car. And
                                              1.   **2.**

I want ___a___ new job, but not in ___an___ office.
     3.   **4.**

We need _____ money for _____ food. We pay _____ high rent. We want
       5.   **6.**   **7.**

___a___ new furniture. I want ___a___ radio.
8.   **9.**

We have two _____ children. I have _____ mother and _____ father. They
          10.   **11.**   **12.**

live with us. We can't live in ___an___ apartment. We need _____ more room.
                        13.   **14.**

We want ___a___ house.
     15.

I don't like ___✗___ my roommates. They play ___a___ loud music all day.
         16.   **17.**

Their friends come over on Saturdays. They have _____ parties. I can't stand
                                          18.

_____ noise. Problems, problems, problems!
19.

			have	a problem.
I		can't	come	to class.
We		don't	help	me.
People				

	Do	you	speak	English?
Where	do	you	study?	
When	can	they	take	a class?
Why	don't	you	practice?	

Where?   **When?**

here	on the bus	now	on Tuesday
there	on Elm Street	at 9:00	from Monday
at school	in a store	at night	to Friday
at home	in an office	in the morning	all day

Why? Because _____ .

C. Make questions with these words and words of your own. Answer them and add more information.

EXAMPLE: **a:** Do you have problems with work?
b: No, I don't. I work in a store and I like it a lot.

Do you   have problems with
- your house or apartment?
- school or work?
- money?
- your English?
- _____?

Where / When   do you
- work?
- practice English?
- _____?

Where   do you   go
- on Wednesdays?
- in the afternoon?
- _____?

Why   can't / don't   you
- learn more job skills?
- get a (better) job?
- move to a better place?
- _____?

What   do   you   do
- at your job?
- in the afternoon?
- on the weekends?
- _____?

Moving

CHAPTER

3

COMPETENCIES
Telling housing needs
Describing housing problems
Reading and answering housing ads
Asking for housing information
Describing locations of things

GRAMMAR
It and *there*
Some/any
Place prepositions

PART ONE /*It* and *There*: Affirmative Statements

- Telling Housing Needs

There's a great apartment on Pine Street.

It	has	no laundry room.	
It	's	two blocks away.	it's = it is
It	's	big and clean.	
There	's	a new refrigerator.	
There	's	no yard.	there's = there is

A. Make sentences with these words. (Say or write them.)

EXAMPLE: 1. It has **no air conditioning**.
There's **electric heat**.
And it's **expensive**.

It has ___no stove___ . sive
There's ___an old refrigerator___
And it's ___too small___ .

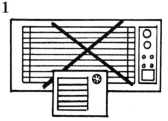

1

no air conditioning
electric heat
expensive

2.

no stove
an old refrigerator
too small

3.

no yard
no laundry room
a mile to the laundromat

B. Choose the correct words.

1. [~~There~~ / There's] a great apartment on Pine Street. 2. [It / It's] has a big kitchen.

3. [There / (There's)] a nice refrigerator. 4. [It / (It's)] new. 5. [(It) / There] has an electric

6. stove, and [it's / (there's)] gas heat. 7. [It's / (There's)] air conditioning, too. 8. [(It) / There]

9. has security, and [(it's) / there's] safe. 10. [(It's) / There] in a nice neighborhood, and

11. [it / (there's)] a bus stop only a block away.

Singular	There's	a parking garage.
	There's	no security.
Plural	There are	carpets and drapes.
	There are	no trees.

C. Make sentences with these words.

EXAMPLE: **1.** There's **a laundry room**.   There's ___*nice furniture*___ .
                There are **four washers and dryers**. There are ___*new carpets and*___ .
                                                               drapes

1.

a laundry room
four washers and
       dryers

2.

nice furniture
new carpets and
       drapes

3.

enough room for cars
two spaces for us in
    the parking garage

D. Choose the correct words.

I can't stand this place! [~~There~~ / **There are**] no elevators. [**There's** / There are]
                                        1.   **2.**

electric heat, and [**it's** / there's] expensive. [**There's** / There are] no air conditioning,
                        3.   **4.**

and [**it's** / there's] hot in the afternoon. [There's / **There are**] no trees or grass.
        5.   **6.**

[**There's** / There are] no transportation. [There's / **There are**] no bus stops nearby.
7.   **8.**

[**It's** / There's] in a bad neighborhood, and [there's / **there are**] no shopping centers.
9.   **10.**

| The | house | has | five rooms. | = | There | are | five rooms | in the house. |
| | It | has | no heat. | = | There | 's | no heat. | |

E. Make sentences with the same meanings. Use *there's* and *there are*.

EXAMPLE: **1. a:** The house has five rooms. =
     b: There are five rooms in the house.

House for Rent

1. The house has five rooms. _There are five rooms in the house_

2. It has two bedrooms. _There are two bedrooms in the house_

3. It has a big kitchen. _There's a big kitchen in the house_

4. It has electric heat. _There's an electric heat in the house_

5. It has no air conditioning. _There's no air conditioning_

6. It has no drapes. _There are no drapes_

But let's look at it! _____

*F. Make sentences about the house in the picture on the next page. Use these words and words of your own.

EXAMPLES: **1. a:** It's **big and clean**.   **1.** It's (not) _bus stop_ .
     b: It's **not near a shopping center**.
    2. a: There's **a big kitchen**.   **2.** There's (no) _dining room_ .
     b: There's **no garage**.
    3. a: There are **five rooms**.   **3.** There are (no) _shopping centers_ .
     b: There are **no drapes**.

big and clean	five rooms	a dishwasher	carpets
expensive	two bedrooms and	laundry room	drapes
near a shopping	two bathrooms	elevators	a yard
center	a big kitchen	furniture	grass
in a nice	a gas stove	electric heat	trees
neighborhood	a refrigerator	air conditioning	parking

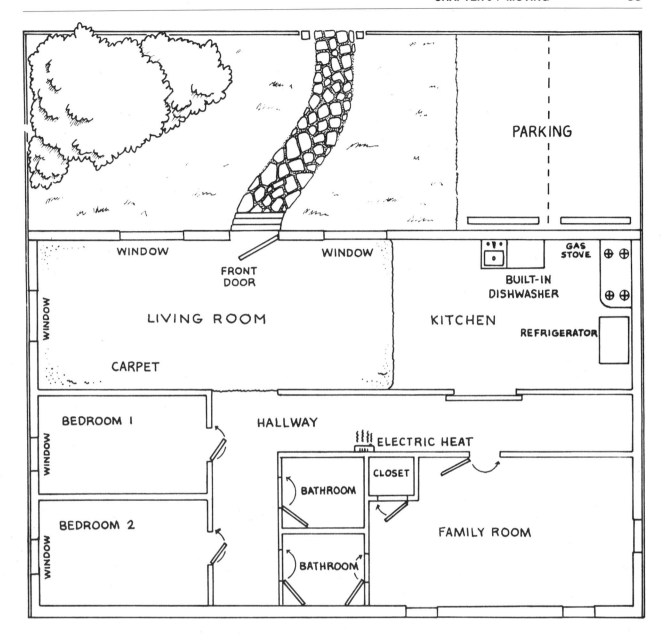

*Now finish the sentences in F with information about your house or apartment. (Say or write them.)

EXAMPLES:
1. It's a small house on a quiet street.
2. It's not far from school.
3. There's a family room.
4. There's no air conditioning.
5. There are trees and flowers.
6. There are no bus stops nearby.

G. **Tell or write about the perfect house or apartment for you. (You can work in small groups.)

EXAMPLE: It's in a safe neighborhood near shopping and transportation. There are good schools for our children.

PART TWO   *It* and *There*: Negative Statements; *A/An*; *Some/Any*

● Describing Housing Problems

There isn't any hot water.

This place needs some repairs. There's a broken window. It's cold in here. There isn't any heat in the morning, and there's no hot water in the afternoon. There aren't any lights in the hall. It's noisy. And there are bugs.

Do you need a plumber, an electrician, or an exterminator?

All of them.

Sorry, but there aren't any repairpeople available now.

There aren't any broken windows here. There's enough heat. There's hot water all day. There isn't any noise, and there aren't any bugs.

But there aren't any children, and there are no pets!

ADULTS
NO PETS

APARTMENT MANAGER

It's not noisy. = It isn't noisy.	There's no heat. = There isn't any heat.	There are no bugs. = There aren't any bugs.
isn't = is not		aren't = are not

A. Finish the sentences with these words. (Say or write them.)

EXAMPLE: 1. **It** isn't quiet.

There's	There	It's	It

I hate this apartment. **It** isn't quiet. **it's** not clean. **there** isn't any hot
1.   2.   3.

water in the morning. **there's** no heat at night. **there** isn't any security. **there's**
4.   5.   6.

no garage. **it's** not safe here. **it** isn't comfortable.
7.   8.

's	isn't	aren't

I love this place. It **isn't** noisy. It **'s** not dirty. There **aren't** any broken
9.   10.   11.

windows. There **aren't** any bugs. There **'s** no elevator. But that's O.K. It **isn't**
12.   13.   14.

expensive. And there **aren't** any problems!
15.

there's	There	there	isn't	aren't

But **there's** no yard. **There** **aren't** any trees around the place. **There**
16.   17.   18.   19.

isn't any room for pets, and **there** **aren't** any children in the building. **There**
20.   21.   22.   23.

aren't any schools in the neighborhood. It's not the place for us!
24.

	Yes	No	Questions
Singular a/an	Call an electrician.	We don't need a plumber.	Is there a problem?
Plural some/any	We need some new pipes. (or: We need new pipes.)	There aren't any lights.	Are there any trees? (or: Are there trees?)
Noncount some/any	There's some room for bikes. (or: There's room for bikes.)	There isn't any noise.	Do you have any wire? (or: Do you have wire?)

B. Make sentences with these words.

EXAMPLES: **1.** There are **some problems**, and it isn't **comfortable here**. We need **some hot water**.

There ['s / **are**] <u>some bugs</u>, and it isn't <u>clean in the kitchen</u> We need <u>an exterminator</u>

1.

some problems
comfortable here
some hot water

2.

some bugs
clean in the kitchen
an exterminator

3.

a broken window
safe in the hall
some new glass

EXAMPLES: **4.** There isn't **any heat in this room**. It's **too cold**. Can we get **an electric heater**?

There [**isn't** / aren't] _____ .
It's _____ .
Can we get _____ ?

4.

any heat in this room
too cold
an electric heater

5.

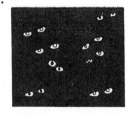

any lights here
dangerous
some light bulbs

6.

any music in this house
too quiet
a radio

C. Choose the correct words.

I can't stand this apartment. There aren't [~~some~~ / any] big windows. I want
                                                         1.

[a / some] sunlight in the morning. And there isn't [some / any] heat in the afternoon.
2.   **3.**

Why don't we have [a / any] hot water at night? The place has [an / any] old
                   4.   **5.**

refrigerator. There isn't [a / any] room for our cars. I have [a / some] big car and
                          6.   **7.**

I can't find [some / any] parking.
             8.

*D. Choose words and have conversations of your own about your house or apartment.

EXAMPLE: At my place there's room for cars on the street, but we really need a parking garage. And we don't have any security.

b: Well, we have security, but there aren't any children in the building. I want a place with families.

a: At my place | there's / there are | a / an / some | _____ , but we need | a / an / some | _____ .

And we don't have _____ .

b: Well, we have | a / an / some | _____ , but there | isn't / aren't | any _____ .

I want | a / an / some | _____ .

**E. Answer these questions: Do you have any problems with housing? What are they? What can you do about them? How can you fix them? Who can you call? (You can work in small groups.)

PART THREE / *It* and *There*: Questions and Answers

● Reading and Answering Housing Ads ● Asking for Housing Information

How many rooms are there?

a: Can you tell me about the house for rent, please? How many bedrooms are there?

b: There are four bedrooms and two and a half baths. And there's a dining room, too.

a: Oh, really? Well, how many stories are there?

b: It's a two-story house. There's a basement, too.

a: Wow! Is it furnished?

b: Yes, it is. It has beautiful furniture.

a: Is there any parking?

b: Yes, there is. There's room for two cars in the garage. It's in back of the house.

a: Are there a washing machine and dryer?

b: No, there aren't. But there's enough room for them in the basement.

a: Oh, good. Is there a dishwasher?

b: No, there isn't.

a: Is there a swimming pool?

b: Sure there is—in the park eight blocks away.

a: Is there a game room?

b: Yes, next to the swimming pool in the park. Sir, we have a house for rent—not a club!

| Is it a furnished apartment? | Yes, it is. |
| | No, it isn't. |

Is there a dining room?			is.
Is there any parking?	Yes,		are.
		there	's not.
Are there carpets and drapes?	No,		isn't.
Are there any washing machines?			aren't.

| How many rooms are there? | There are (number). |

A. Make questions with these words. Finish the answers with information from the housing ad. (Say or write them.)

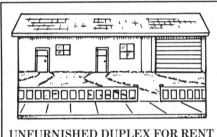

UNFURNISHED DUPLEX FOR RENT
Large, 3 bedrooms, 1-1/2 baths, garage.

EXAMPLES:
1. a: Is there a house for rent?
   b: No, there isn't. It's a duplex.
2. a: Is it large?
   b: Yes, it is.

1. _Is there a house for rent_ No, _there isn't_ .
   a house for rent / Is / there / ?
   It's _a duplex_ .

2. _Is it large?_ Yes, _it is._ .
   it / large / Is / ?

3. _How many bedrooms are there_ There _are three bedrooms_ .
   bedrooms / are / there / How many / ?

4. _Are there two bathrooms?_ No, _there aren't_ .
   Are / two bathrooms / there / ?
   There _are 1½ bathrooms_ .

5. _Is there a garage?_ Yes, _there is_ .
   there / Is / a garage / ?

6. _Is it furnished?_ No, _it isn't_ .
   furnished / it / Is / ?
   It's _unfurnished_ .

7. _Are there carpets and drapes?_ No, _there aren't_ .
   carpets and drapes / Are / there / ?

8. _How many stories Are there_ There _are one story_ .
   How many / there / are / stories / ?

B. Finish the questions with these words. Answer them with information from the housing ad.

EXAMPLES: a: Is there a house for rent?
            b: No, there isn't. But there's an apartment.

> **FURNISHED APARTMENT**
> **FOR RENT**
> 2 bedrooms, stove, refrigerator. Gas heat.

Is	Are	are	there	it

1. _Is_ _there_ a house for rent?

2. _Is_ _it_ furnished? (_Is_ _it_ furniture?)

3. How many bedrooms _are_ _there_ ?

4. _Are_ _there_ a stove and a refrigerator?

5. _Is_ _there_ electric heat?

*C. Make questions with these words and words of your own. Answer them with information from the housing ads on page 47.

EXAMPLES: 1. a: Is there a furnished apartment for rent?
               b: No, there's not. It's unfurnished.
               a: How many bedrooms are there?
               b: There's one, and one bath.

Is
Are | there | a
              an
              any | apartment for rent?
                    house for sale?
                    room available?
                    big kitchen?
                    electric range?
                    room for cars?
                    carpets and drapes?
                    washer and dryer?
                    swimming pool?
                    _____ ?

Is it | large / big / small?
        expensive / new / old?
        comfortable / clean / dirty?
        on the [first / second] floor?
        furnished / unfurnished?
        near [shopping / transportation] ?
        in a [safe / nice] neighborhood?
        quiet / noisy?
        _____ ?

How many | stories
           rooms
           bedrooms
           bathrooms
           _____ | are there?

1	UNFURNISHED APARTMENT FOR RENT

$430 1 bedroom, 1 bath.
Second floor. Large kitchen.
Gas range and heat. Carpets,
drapes. Laundry room.

3	MOBILE HOME FOR SALE

$35,000. Living room, 2
bedrooms, 1 bath. Stove,
refrigerator. In beautiful
park with trees and flowers,
pool and game room.
CHILDREN AND PETS WELCOME.

2	TOWNHOUSE FOR RENT

$950/month. 3-stories,
3 bedrooms, 2 1/2 baths.
Family room. 2-car garage.
Basement, washer, dryer.
Built-ins with dishwasher.
Air conditioning.

4	FURNISHED ROOM FOR RENT

$280/month in 4-bedroom
apartment. Private bath
and telephone. Parking space
in garage.

**D. Look at housing ads in your local newspaper. Ask and answer questions about them. (You can work in small groups.)

*E. Choose words and have conversations about your house or apartment.

EXAMPLES:
a: Is there an elevator in your building?
b: No, there isn't. There are only two stories.
a: Is it a large building?
b: Yes, it is. There are thirty apartments.
a: How many rooms are there in your apartment?
b: There are five—a living room, a dining room, a kitchen, and two bedrooms.

a: [Is / (Are)] there [a / an / (any)] ___pets___ in your [house / apartment / building] ?

b: [Yes, / (No,)] there [is(n't) / (are(n't))] .

a: Is it _____ ?

b: [Yes, / No,] it [is / isn't] .

a: How many ___bedrooms___ are there in ___your apartment___ ?

b: There are ___a living room and kitchen___ .

**F. Tell or write about another student's house or apartment.

EXAMPLE: Coco's building has two stories, but there are no children.

PART FOUR / Place Prepositions; Review

● Describing Locations of Things

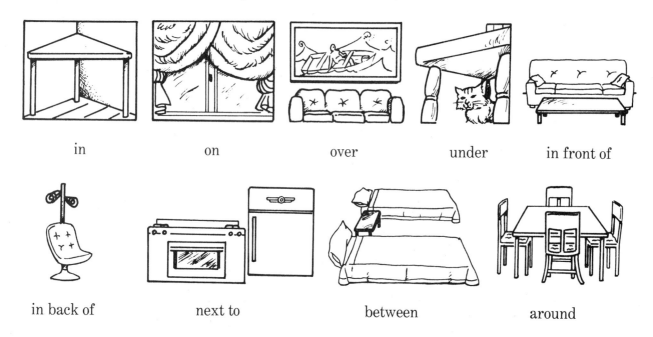

in   on   over   under   in front of

in back of   next to   between   around

A. Make sentences about the above pictures. Say or write them.

EXAMPLES: a: There's a table in the corner.
            b: There are drapes on the window.

B. Make sentences about this picture. Say or write them.

EXAMPLES: a: There's a couch in the living room.
            b: It's between two tables.
            a: There's a coffee table in front of the couch.

It	's	a nice place.	
It	isn't	expensive.	
	There	's	no furniture	in the bedroom.
	There	isn't	any hot water	in the bathroom.
	There	are	two clocks	in my living room.
	There	aren't	any parks	near the place.
Is	there		a refrigerator?
Are	there		any children	in the building?
How many		apartments	are there?

*C. **Play a conversation game. Ask and answer questions and add information.**

a: Look only at Picture 1.   **b:** Look only at Picture 2.

Write X on the differences between the two pictures.

EXAMPLES: **a:** Are there two pictures over the couch in Picture 2?
b: Yes, there are. And there's a map next to them. Is there a map in Picture 1?
a: No, there's not. How many tables are there in the living room?

D. **Ask and answer questions about things in your house or apartment. (You can work in small groups.)**

EXAMPLES: **a:** Is there a T.V. set in your living room?
b: Yes, there is. And there's a set in the bedroom, too.

Food and Things

COMPETENCIES:
Expressing possession
Describing feelings and places
Making suggestions
Asking about food and restaurants
Describing restaurants

GRAMMAR:
Possessive forms
The verb *be*
Two-word verbs

PART ONE   Possessive Forms; Nouns, Pronouns, and Adjectives

● Expressing Possession

This is our new house.

That ese those
this-este these estos

This is That's	my our your his her their	game.	These are Those are	my our your his her their	games.

A. Make sentences for the pictures with these words.

EXAMPLES: 1. This is **my** bed. That's **your** bed.
2. These are **our** toys. Those are **their** toys.

1.
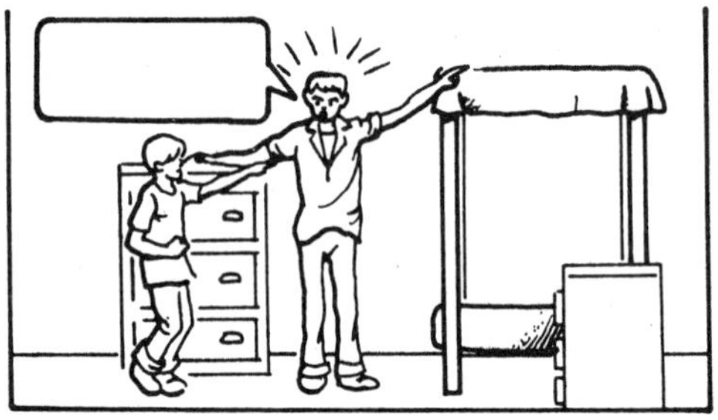

2.
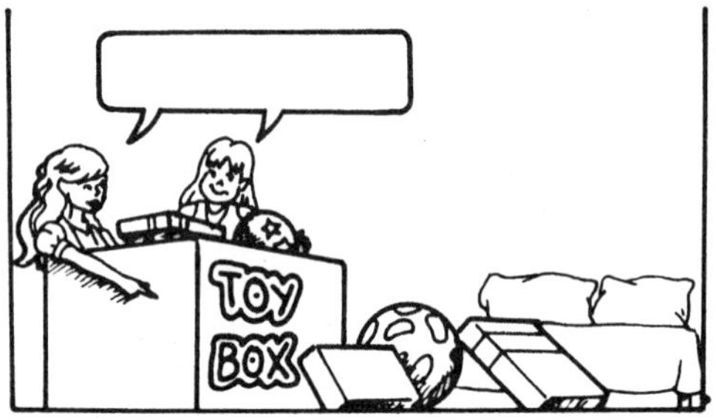

bed	chest of drawers	blankets

toys	ball	games

B. Find the things for the people. Then make sentences about them with the words.

EXAMPLE: 1. This is **his** jacket.

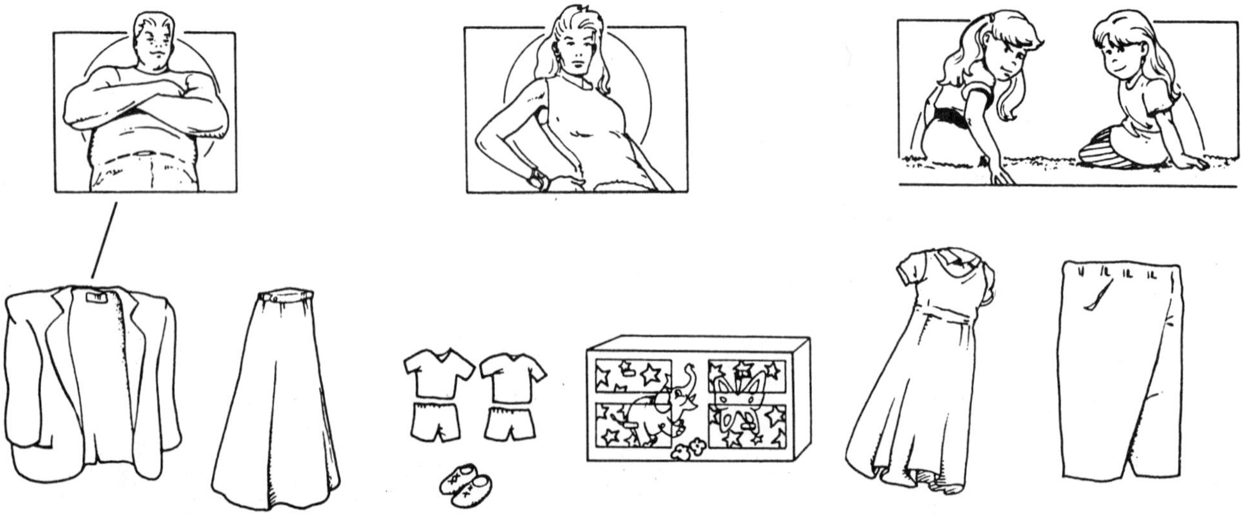

1. jacket 2. skirt 3. clothes 4. chest 5. dress 6. pants

8:00 to 10:00
8:00 to 10:00
8:00   9:00

This is	my			This	jacket	is	mine.
That's	our	jacket		That			ours.
These are	your		=	These			yours.
Those are	his			Those	pants	are	his.
	her	pants					hers.
	their						theirs.

C. Make sentences with the same meanings.

EXAMPLE: **1. a:** This is **my** skirt. =
 b: This skirt is **mine**.

1. _this is my skirt._ = This skirt is **mine**.

2. That's **my** sweater. = _That sweater is mine._

3. _That's your blouse._ = That blouse is **yours**.

4. This is **your** jacket. = _This jacket is yours._

Why can't Chris hang up **his** things?

5. _Those are his shirts._ = Those shirts are **his**.

6. These are **his** pants. = _These pants are his._

And how about the girls?

7. _These are their clothes._ = These clothes are **theirs**.

8. This is **their** toy box. = _This toy box is theirs_

Where's Lisa?

9. _Those are her toys._ = Those toys are **hers**.

10. That's **her** blanket. = _That blanket is hers._

11. _This's our furniture._ = This furniture is **ours**.

12. This is **our** new house. = _This new house is ours._

> This is Lisa's coat.   =   This coat is Lisa's.
> That's Edgar and Maria's room.   =   That room is Edgar and Maria's.
> These are the boys' clothes.   =   These clothes are the boys'.

D. Make sentences about the pictures with these words.

EXAMPLES: 1. Those are **Chris's** shoes.   *or*   Those shoes are **Chris's**.

1. Chris

| shoes | shirt | pants |

2. The Girls

| table | chairs | beds |

3. Mark and Lisa

| pencils | paper | picture |

4. Maria

| dishes | bowls | cups |

E. Finish these sentences about things in the classroom. Change the last student's sentence. Then add a new sentence. (You can work in small groups.)

EXAMPLES: a: These are **my** notebooks.
           b: Those notebooks are **yours**. That's **the school's** clock.
           c: That clock is **the school's**. This is **her** bookbag.

1. This is _my pencil_ .

2. This (THING) is _mine_ .

3. That's _your book_ .

4. That (THING) is _his_ .

5. These are _your papers_ .

6. These (THINGS) are _ours._ .

7. Those are _my pants_ .

8. Those (THINGS) are _hers_ .

PART TWO

The Verb *Be*: All Present Forms in Statements

● Describing Feelings and Places ● Making Suggestions

We're hungry! Let's have lunch.

Singular / Noncount					Plural			
The table	is	clean.			The tables	are	dirty.	
Milk	is	good for you.			Soft drinks	are	bad for you.	
I	am	=	I'm		We	are	=	we're	
He	is	=	he's		You	are	=	you're	thirsty.
She	is	=	she's	hungry.	They	are	=	they're	
It	is	=	it's						

A. Finish the sentences with these words and word parts. (Say or write them.)

EXAMPLE: 1. I'**m** very hungry.

'm	is	's	are	're

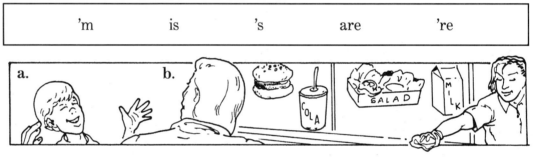

a: I __'m__ very hungry. I can eat a lot of hamburgers.
   1.

b: I know. But hamburgers __are__ bad for you. How about a salad?
              2.

Salads __are__ good for you.
   3.

a: They __'re__ terrible. I want three hamburgers and two cold soft drinks.
     4.

I __'m__ very thirsty. What about Chris? He __'s__ thirsty, too.
5.   **6.**

b: But soft drinks __are__ bad for you. Milk __is__ good. And it __'s__
       7.   **8.**   **9.**
cold, too.

a: We don't want milk. We __'re__ not that thirsty. But we __'re__ very
            10.   **11.**

hungry. What about Lisa? She __'s__ hungry, too.
         12.

Singular / Noncount				Plural			
The table	isn't	clean.			The tables	aren't	clean.
Candy	isn't	healthy.			Soft drinks	aren't	healthy.

				I		'm not	
He (She, It)	isn't		=	He (She, It)		's not	hungry.
We (You, They)	aren't		=	We (You, They)		're not	

B. Finish the sentences with these words or word parts.

EXAMPLE: 1. We**'re** not sure.

isn't	aren't	'm	's	're

Where can we eat? We __'re___ not sure. These places __'re___ very good. And the
                        1.   **2.**

food __is___ cheap. Where's your mother? She __'s___ not here! The food at that place
      3.   **4.**

__isn't___ bad. But I __is___ not happy about the prices. They __'re___ not low. Where
5.   **6.**   **7.**

are the girls? They __aren't___ here.
                      8.

C. Make one or two sentences with the opposite meaning.

1. It's nice here.   It isn't nice here.   It's not nice here.

2. The food here is good.   The food here isn't good   The food here is not good

3. But it's expensive.   But it isn't expensive.   But it's not expensive.

4. The tables and chairs are clean.   They aren't clean.   They're not clean.

5. They're comfortable.   They aren't comfortable.   They're not comfortable.

6. I'm hungry.   I'm not hungry

D. Have conversations with these words.

EXAMPLE: **a:** Let's have **hamburgers**.

          b: No, let's not.
             They aren't
             good for you.
             How about **a steak**?

          a: No, thanks. **It's** too
             too expensive. Let's have
             _____ .

a: Let's have _____ .

b: No, let's not.
    [It / They] [isn't / aren't]
    good for you.
    How about _____ ?

a: No, thanks. [It's / They're]
    expensive. Let's have
    fried chicken.

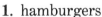

1. hamburgers

2. a steak

3. fried chicken

4. a big salad

5. potato chips

6. some baked potatoes

7. soft drinks

8. a milk shake

9. apple pie

10. some fruit

*11. (a food of
     your own)

*12. (a food of
     your own)

*E. Make sentences from these words and words of your own.

EXAMPLES: **a:** I like chicken because it's not expensive.
               b: I don't like fried chicken because it's not good for you.

I (don't) like	restaurants chicken salads potato chips soft drinks milk _____	because	it's they're	(not)	expensive. cheap. good for you. bad for you. _____

I'm We('re) (Name) He('s) She('s) My classmates They('re) _____	(not) is(n't) are(n't)	cold. hot. hungry. thirsty. tired. _____	I (don't) need We (don't) want Let's (not) get	a sweater. jackets. lunch. [some / any] food. [some / any] fruit. [some / any] drinks. [some / any] coffee. _____

PART THREE / The Verb *Be*: Questions and Answers

Asking about Food and Restaurants

How's the food here?

Am	I	right?		you	are.
Is	the food	homemade?		it	is.
Is	Chris	thirsty?	Yes,	he	is.
Are	you	hungry?		I	am.
Are	the salads	fresh?		they	are.

No,	I'm not.					
	he	(she, it)	isn't	=	he	(she, it)'s not.
	we	(you, they)	aren't	=	we	(you, they)'re not.

Is	the soup	canned or homemade?	It's canned.
Are	the vegetables	fresh or frozen?	They're frozen.

A. **Make questions from these words. Finish the answers with information from the menu. (Say or write them.)**

EXAMPLE:　**1. a:** Is the soup homemade?
　　　　　　　b: Yes, it is.

MENU

Homemade Soup $1.25
Fried Chicken 3.45
Baked Potato .... .95

1. _Is the soup homemade?_　　　Yes, _it's._
　　the soup / homemade / Is / ?

2. _Is it expensive?_　　　No, _it isn't._
　　Is / expensive / it / ?

3. _Is the chicken fried or baked?_It's _fried._
　　fried or baked / the chicken / Is / ?

4. _Are the potatoes mashed or baked?_They're _baked._
　　the potatoes / Are / mashed or baked / ?

5. _Is there fish on the menu?_　　No, _there isn't_
　　on the menu / fish / Is / there / ?

6. _Are you hungry now?_　　　Yes, _I'm._
　　you / hungry now / Are / ?

7. _Is our waitress nearby?_　　No, _she isn't_
　　Is / nearby / our waitress / ?

One hundred and ninety two dollars twelve cents

B. Ask questions for these answers.

EXAMPLES: 1. a: Is the fish fresh?
            b: The fish? Yes, it's fresh.
          2. a: Are the roast beef sandwiches hot or cold?
            b: They're hot. They don't have cold roast beef sandwiches.

Fresh Fish	$6.50
Hot Beef Sandwich	3.25
Fresh Vegetables	1.25
Mashed Potatoes	1.25
Small Salad	1.25
Pie (Apple)	1.95
Coffee (Regular or Decaffeinated)	.85

1. *Is the fish fresh*
   The fish? Yes, it's fresh.

2. *Do they have cold roast beef sandwich*
   They're hot. They don't have cold roast beef sandwiches.

3. *Are the vegetables frozen?*
   No, the vegetables aren't frozen.

4. *Are the big salads on the or decaf menu?*
   They're small. There are no big salads on the menu.

5. *Are you very hungry?*
   No, I'm not very hungry.

6. *Do they have a apple pie*
   Yes, they have apple pie.

7. *Are the potatoes fried*
   No, the potatoes aren't fried.

8. *Is the pie homemade?*
   No, the pie isn't homemade.

9. *Is the coffee regular or decaf*
   It's both. You can have regular or decaf coffee.

10. *Is chris cold?*
    Chris? Yes, he's cold. He needs his jacket.

What	's	this?		what's	=	what is
Who	's	our waiter?		who's	=	who is
Whose coat	is	that?				
Where	are	our menus?		where's	=	where is
When	's	the place	open?	when's	=	when is
Why	aren't	you	thirsty?	why's	=	why is
How	are	the pies	here?	how's	=	how is
How much	is	it?				

C. Make questions with these words. Then find the answers.

EXAMPLE: 1. a: How's the food in this place?
                 b: It's O.K.

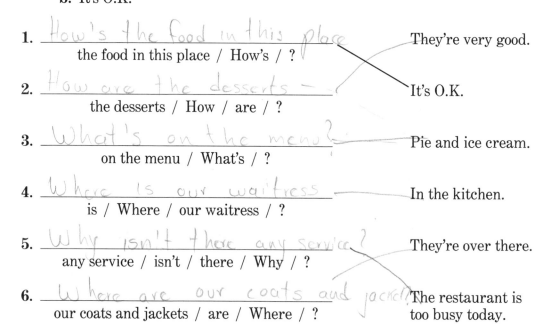

1. _How's the food in this place_   They're very good.
    the food in this place / How's / ?

2. _How are the desserts —_   It's O.K.
    the desserts / How / are / ?

3. _What's on the menu?_   Pie and ice cream.
    on the menu / What's / ?

4. _Where is our waitress_   In the kitchen.
    is / Where / our waitress / ?

5. _Why isn't there any service?_   They're over there.
    any service / isn't / there / Why / ?

6. _Where are our coats and jackets_   The restaurant is
    our coats and jackets / are / Where / ?   too busy today.

D. Read the answers. Then finish the questions with these words and word parts.

EXAMPLE: 1. a: **Whose** are they?   **These aren't
                 b: The last customer's.   our cigarettes.**

| What | Who | Whose | Where | How | Why | 's |

1. _Who_ are they?   The last customer's.

2. _What's_ the special of the day?   Chicken pie.

3. Oh, really? _How_ is it?   Very good.

4. _How_ much is the special? $4.95.

5. _Whose_ the cook tonight?   Mario.

6. _Where's_ our water, please?   Over there. I can get it for you.

7. _Why_ the place so busy?   Because it's Saturday.

_____ *E. Choose words and use words of your own. Finish these questions. Answer them with information from the menu.

EXAMPLES:
1. a: Is the chicken baked?
   b: No, it isn't. It's fried.
2. a: Are the potatoes mashed or baked?
   b: They're mashed.
3. a: What's pie a la mode?
   b: It's pie with ice cream.
4. a: How's the roast beef?
   b: I don't know, but the hot sandwiches aren't expensive.
5. a: How much is coffee?
   b: It's $ .70.

1. [(Is) / Are] _the chicken fried_____ ?

2. [(Is) / Are] _the fish baked_ or _broiled_____ ?

3. What [is / ('s) / are] _the menu for lunch_____ ?

4. How [is / ('s) / are] _the coffee,_____ ?

5. How much [is / ('s) / are] _the pie a la Mode_ ?

DINNERS

(with homemade soup, mashed potatoes
or french fries, and a fresh vegetable)

Fried Chicken $4.15
Steak 6.85
Fish (Baked or Broiled) 5.50

SALADS		SANDWICHES	
Large	2.45	Hamburger	2.85
Small	1.50	Hot Roast Beef	3.20
		Chicken (Cold)	2.40

DRINKS		DESSERTS	
Milk	.85	Ice Cream (Vanilla or Chocolate)	1.25
Coffee	.70	Pie (Apple or Cherry)	1.85
Tea (Hot or Iced)	.85	Pie à la Mode	2.10
Hot Chocolate	.85	Cake	1.65
Soft Drinks	.70		

_____ **F. Get real menus from restaurants and bring them to class. Ask and answer questions about them. (You can work in small groups.)

PART FOUR / Two-Word Verbs; Review

- Describing Restaurants

come back	put away	get on	go out	hang up	colgar
come in	get up	get off	go back	sit down	

A. Finish the questions with these words. Say or write them in sentences and add information.

EXAMPLE: **1. a:** Do you go **out** to restaurants?   **b:** Yes, I do. I go out to restaurants..

back	out	up	down

1. Do you go ____out____ to restaurants?

2. Do you hang ____up____ your coat or jacket there?

3. Do you sit ____down____ at the counter?

4. Do you always go ____back____ to the same place?

B. Finish the sentences with these words.

come back	get off	go out	sit down
come in	get on	hang up	put away

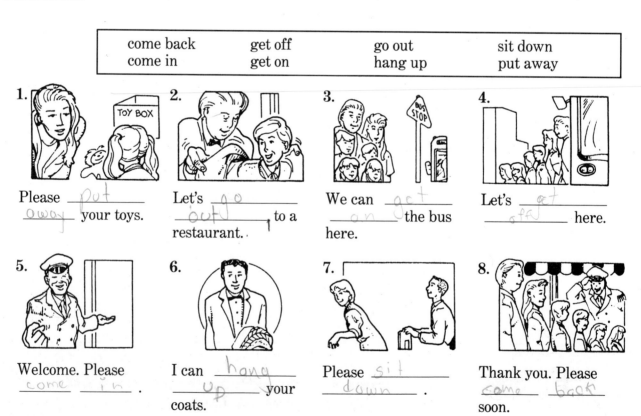

1. Please ___put___ ___away___ your toys.

2. Let's ___go___ ___out___ to a restaurant.

3. We can ___get___ ___on___ the bus here.

4. Let's ___get___ ___off___ here.

5. Welcome. Please ___come___ ___in___ .

6. I can ___hang___ ___up___ your coats.

7. Please ___sit___ ___down___ .

8. Thank you. Please ___come___ ___back___ soon.

Whose	(soup)	is	this?		It's	my our your his her their	soup. fries.		It's	mine. ours. yours. his. hers. theirs.
	(fries)	are	these?		They're				They're	

C. Have conversations for this picture.

EXAMPLES: **a:** Whose chicken dinner is that?
b: It's Lisa's. It's hers.

		I	'm not	hungry.
		You	're	right.
		The waitress	isn't	very fast.
		She	's	busy.
	Are	the tables		clean?
What	's	that		in your glass?
Who	's	our waiter?		
Whose table	is	this?		
Where	is	he?		
How	's	your hamburger?		
How much	are	the french fries?		
Why	aren't	you		hungry anymore?

watch out
look out
go out
hang up
sit down
stand up
listen to
tose away.

Put { away
      on
      down
      up — with
      off — delay

_____ *D. **Choose words and use words of your own. Ask and answer questions about your favorite restaurant.**

EXAMPLES: 1. a: What's the name of the place?
                 b: It's the Rose Cafe.

1. What's the name of the place?

2. Who's | the owner?
          | the cook?
          | your favorite [waiter / waitress] ?   Is | he | fast?
                                                                    | she | friendly?

3. Is the service | fast?   Why or why not?
                   | good?

4. What's | your favorite | food?
    What are | | foods?

5. Where's the restaurant?   When's it open?

6. How's the food?   Is it expensive?

7. How much is a good | lunch?
                       | dinner?
                       | dessert?

8. Is | (there) any_____ ?   11. Who | is | your favorite?
    Are | What | are |

9. Where | is | your favorite? drink?   12. How (much) | is | a good dinner.
    When | are | | are |

10. Why | is(n't) | our waiter ?
        | are(n't) |

_____ **E. **Tell or write about another student's favorite restaurant or try a new restaurant. Tell the class about it. Answer questions. (You can work in small groups.)**

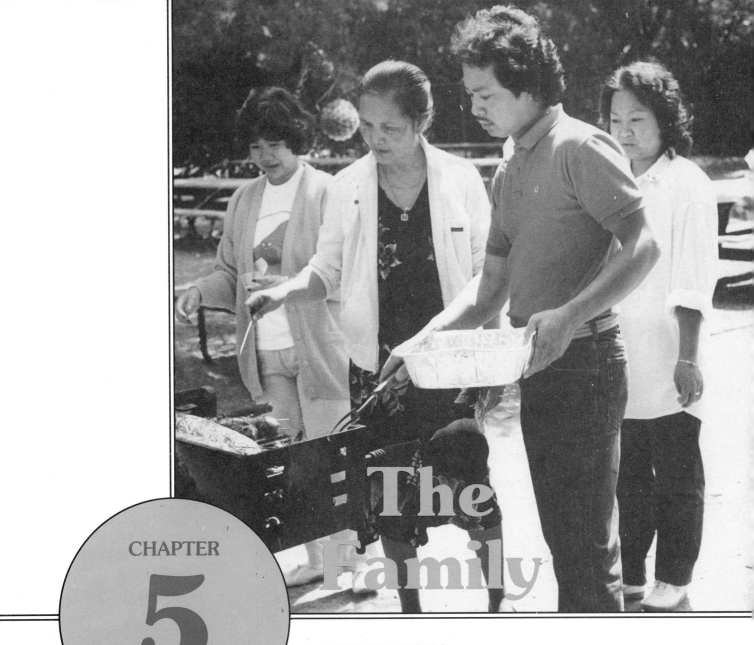

CHAPTER 5

The Family

COMPETENCIES:
Describing and telling about people
Asking about families
Using the telephone
Describing family activities

GRAMMAR:
The simple present (the -s ending)
Infinitives after verbs
Frequency words
Indirect objects

PART ONE   The Simple Present: The -s Ending; Statements; Infinitives after Verbs

● Describing and Telling about People

Do you miss your family too?

My parents live in an apartment in Paris. My father wants to move. But my mother doesn't. She doesn't want a big house.

My sister lives in a small town. She has to work in a factory, and she doesn't like her job. Her husband drives a bus.

Their children go to school. My niece writes letters, but my nephew doesn't. I send them presents. I want to visit them.

My favorite aunt is a teacher. She knows Spanish, but she doesn't know English. She wants to come here with her daughter on vacation.

Uh-huh. I see. How interesting. You sure have a lot of relatives.

Oh, yes, and I have more pictures.

I miss my brother Louis. He works for a newspaper. He's very interesting.

My brother Alan calls me every week. And this is my uncle Paul. He's a cook. And look . . . some cousins.

| I | | like | to | get | letters. |
| She | doesn't | have | to | work. | |

These words can come before *to*:

| want | like | love | need | have |

D. Add *to* and finish the sentences with these words.

EXAMPLE: 1. My mother doesn't need **to work**.

1. My mother doesn't need _to work_ . (work).

2. She likes _to stay_ home. (stay)

3. My two brothers love _to travel_. (travel)

4. My sister wants _to have_ more children. (have)

5. But she has _to make_ more money. (make)

E. Finish the sentences with forms of these words. Add *to* if necessary.

EXAMPLES: 1. My girlfriend **wants to** come to this country.
2. But her family **needs** money.

1. My girlfriend _wants_ come to this country. (want)

2. But her family _needs_ money. (need)

3. And she _doesn't have_ any vacation time. (not have)

4. So she _has_ work. (have)

5. She _doesn't like_ her job. (not like)

6. But she _loves_ me. (love)

7. I _likes_ be with her. (like)

8. I _needs_ visit her. (need)

9. But I _don't have_ enough money for a trip. (not have)

All the Time	Now
I don't like my job. He doesn't like to work.	I want a new job. He wants to stay home.

*F.   **Choose words and finish the sentences. You can get ideas from the pictures, but add information of your own, too.**

EXAMPLE: **1.** I like **to drive**, but I don't want **a new car**.

1. I | like / don't like | (to) _____ .

2. I | want / don't want | (to) _____ .

3. My | husband / wife / friend | likes / doesn't like | (to) work. but he doesn't want _____ .

4. He / She | wants / doesn't want | (to) speak English but he doesn't want to study English.

5. My | parents / children / friends | need / don't need | (to) study but they don't want to do their homework

6. They | have / don't have | (to) do their homework but they don't have time for do it

7. My | father / mother | works / doesn't work | in | a / an | store but my mother doesn't work in a store

8. He / She | has / doesn't have | (to) work but he doesn't have car .

G.   **Tell or write about another student and his or her family.

EXAMPLE: Juan likes to drive, but he doesn't want a new car.

PART TWO
The Simple Present: The -s Ending; Yes/No Questions; Frequency Words

● Asking about Families

Do you see your family often?

a: Haruko

b: Cristina

Hmmm ... Nice pictures. Interesting. Tell me more about your family.

a: Does your father work?

b: Yes, he does. He has a clothing store.

a: Oh, really? Does your mother ever help him in the store?

b: She occasionally does, but not often. She usually stays home and takes care of the house. She does dishes and laundry. She's a housewife.

a: How often do you talk to your sister and brother-in-law?

b: About once a month. I write my niece every two weeks, and I like to send them presents a few times a year.

a: Do you ever visit your brothers?

b: Well, I almost never see them, but I sometimes think about them. My brother Louis occasionally calls me long distance. My brother Alan calls more often. My favorite aunt usually calls, too. Let me tell you . . . .

a: Haruko

b: Cristina

O.K., later. Do you want to see pictures of my family? Look, this is our house in Japan. This is my uncle. Here's a picture of my cousins in a restaurant. Here . . .

| Does | your son | live | with you? | Yes, he does. |
| Does | your wife | work? | | No, she doesn't. |

A sentence can have two forms of the word *do*.

Example: Does your mother **do** housework? Yes, she does.

A. Finish the sentences with these words. (Say or write them.)

| Do | Does | does | don't | doesn't |

1. _Does_____ your mother work in a store?   No, she _doesn't_ .

2. _Does_____ she take care of the house?   Yes, she _does_ .

3. _Does_____ your father do dishes, too?   No, he _doesn't_ .

4. _Do_____ your brothers live with your parents?   No, they _don't_ .

B. Have conversations with these words.

EXAMPLE: 1. a: **Do** your **parents work**?   a: [Do / Does] your _brother work_?
                 b: Yes, **they do.**   b: Yes, [they / he / she] _does_ .
                 a: **Does** your **grandfather**?   a: [Do / Does] your _aunt study_ ?
                 b: No, **he doesn't.**   b: No, [they / he / she] _doesn't_ .

a: parents work
a: grandfather

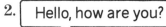

a: father know English
a: mother

a: daughter live with you
a: sons

a: brother have kids
a: sister

a: aunts like to travel
a: uncles

(a conversation
of your own)

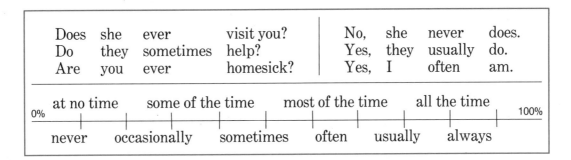

Does	she	ever	visit you?
Do	they	sometimes	help?
Are	you	ever	homesick?

No,	she	never	does.
Yes,	they	usually	do.
Yes,	I	often	am.

0% at no time   some of the time   most of the time   all the time 100%

never   occasionally   sometimes   often   usually   always

C. Make questions and answers with these words.

EXAMPLES: **1. a:** Do you often talk to her?   **b:** No, but I sometimes do.

How about your sister?

1. Do you often talk to her? No, but _I sometimes do_
to her / Do / often / you / talk / ?   do / sometimes / I / .

2. Does she ever call you? Yes, _She occasionally does_
Does / ever / call you / she / ?   occasionally / she / does / .

3. Does she ever visit you? No, _she never does_
visit you / she / Does / ever / ?   does / she / never / .

4. Are you ever homesick? Yes, _I usually am_
homesick / you / Are / ever / ?   usually / am / I / .

D. Make questions and answers with these words and words of your own.

EXAMPLE: **a:** Does your brother ever visit you?   **b:** Yes, he occasionally does.

Do Does	your	parents mother father children son daughter brother(s) sister(s) ___	ever occasionally sometimes often usually	write call visit ___	you?

Yes,	they she he	always often ___	do. does.

No,	they she he	never	do. does.

Are you	ever sometimes ___	homesick?

Yes, I	usually occasionally ___	am.
No, I	never	

How often	do	you		travel?		
How often	does	your son		work?		

once	a day			day
twice	a week			two weeks
three times	a month		every	few months
a few times	a year			other year
_____	_____			_____

E.

Make questions with these words and words of your own. Answer them with information from the calendar.

EXAMPLE: a: How often does your brother call home?
b: He calls home once a week (every Sunday).

How often	do	you	call home?
		your parents	write letters?
		your _____s	visit relatives?
	does	your sister	send presents?
		your _____	ask _____ to dinner?
		_____	

Sun.	Mon.	Tues.	Wed.	Thurs.	Fri.	Sat.
call home		visit relatives	write letters	call aunt		have dinner with father
call home	visit relatives				ask cousins to dinner	
call home		visit relatives	write letters			have dinner with father
call home					send presents	

*Now answer the above questions with information about you.

PART THREE
The Simple Present: The -s Ending
(Questions and Answers)

● Using the Telephone

What does she do first?

Cristina has some relatives in Canada. She often calls them from home. She calls after 11:00 p.m. because the long-distance rates are lower then.

1.

She picks up the receiver and listens for the dial tone.

2.

She dials 1 + her cousin's area code + 555-1212 for local information.

3.

The operator gives Cristina her cousin's telephone number.

4.

She dials 1 + the area code + the telephone number. Her cousin answers.

5.

They talk for an hour.

6.

Cristina gets a telephone bill every month.

1. Where does Cristina call from?

2. When does she call? (Why does she make telephone calls so late?)

3. What does she do first?

4. Why does she dial 1 + the area code + 555-1212?

5. Who gives her information?

6. What number does she call then?

7. Who does she call? (Who answers the phone?)

8. How long do they talk?

9. How often does she get a telephone bill?

10. How much does she have to pay for the call to her cousin?

Who	does	Cristina	call	at night?
What	does	she	do	first?
What number	does	she	dial?	
Where	does	she	get	the number?
Why	doesn't	she	call	earlier?
How long	does	she	talk?	

A. **Read the answers. Then finish the questions with these words. (Say or write them.)**

EXAMPLE: 1. a: <u>**Where does**</u> Cristina sometimes call from?
            b: A public telephone.

does	Who	What	Where	When	How
	Person	time	place	time	

1. _<u>Where</u>_ _<u>does</u>_ Cristina sometimes call from?   A public telephone.

2. _<u>What</u>_ _<u>does</u>_ she do first?   She picks up the receiver.

3. _<u>What</u>_ _<u>does</u>_ she listen for?   The dial tone.

4. _<u>How</u>_ much _<u>does</u>_ she put in the coin slot?   Twenty-five cents.

5. _<u>How</u>_ _<u>does</u>_ she call!?   Direct. (She doesn't ask for the operator's help.)

6. _<u>Who</u>_ _<u>does</u>_ she wait for?   The operator.

7. _<u>Where</u>_ _<u>does</u>_ she put more money?   In the coin slot.

8. _<u>Who</u>_ _<u>does</u>_ she talk to?   Her aunt and uncle.

9. _<u>How</u>_ long _<u>does</u>_ she talk?   For a few minutes.

10. _<u>When</u>_ _<u>does</u>_ she have to put in more money?   After three minutes.

Who	misses	his or her family?
Who	calls	home a lot?
Who	's	homesick?

Compare: Who calls you? / Who do you call?

B. Have conversations with these words.

EXAMPLE: a: Who (in your family) <u>talks on the phone?</u>   a: Who _____ ?
          b: <u>Our daughters (do).</u>   b: _____

In Your Family

1.

a: talks on the phone
b: our daughters

2.

a: writes letters home
b: my son

3.

a: visits relatives
b: we

In Your Class

4.

a: has a big family
b:

5.

a: lives with relatives
b:

6.

a: is homesick
b:

*C. Have conversations of your own about families.

EXAMPLE: a: Who makes the decisions in your family?
          b: My father and mother do.
          a: Who _____ s _____ ?

**D. Tell or write about another student's family.

EXAMPLE: In Gina's family, her grandmother makes the important decisions.

PART FOUR / Indirect Objects; Review

● Describing Family Activities

I	write		letters	(to my family).
They	send		presents	(to me).
We	make		dinner	(for them).

I	write	my family	letters.
They	send	me	presents.
We	make	them	dinner.

bring	give	read	tell
buy	make	show	write

A. Make sentence with these words. (Say or write them.)

EXAMPLE: 1. I like to write my parents letters.

The people in my family are very close.

1. _I like to write my parents letters_
    my parents / I / like to write / letters / .

2. _My sister makes me dinner._
    dinner / me / My sister / makes / .

3. _I give her children presents._
    give / presents / I / her children / .

4. _I read them stories every night_
    I / them / stories / every night / read / .

5. _They want to teach me English._
    want to teach / English / They / me / .

B. Make sentences with the same meanings.

EXAMPLE: 1. a: My niece brings the newspaper **to me** every day. =
            b: My niece brings **me** the newspaper every day.

1. My niece brings the newspaper **to me** every day. = _____
    My niece brings me the newspaper every day

2. I love to tell stories **to her**. = _I love to tell her stories._

3. We often buy toys **for our nephews**. = _We often buy our nephews toys_

4. Look! Let me show some family pictures **to you**. = _Let me show you_
    some family pictures

What	Do	you	have	children?
Why	does	your son	like	to do?
Who	doesn't	he	need	to study?
			speaks	Korean?

| Yes, | I we they | do. | No, | I we they | don't. | Yes, | he she it | does. | No, | he she it | doesn't. |

| Who? | What | do does | _____ | do (all day)? |

Who?

my parents
my best friend
our uncle Jim
my daughters

They do housework.
She takes classes.
He drives a bus.
Play with the children.

| What | do does | _____ | like want need | to do? | Where? | When? |

She wants to study French.
He likes to cook.
They need to make money.
Talk on the telephone.

At home.
On 22nd Street.
To school.
In an office.

On Monday.
In the morning.
In January.
All week.

How often?

Once a month.
Twice a day.
Every weekend.
Every two years.

Why?

(because) I don't have any money.
(because) Our family lives in Tokyo.
(because) He has to look for an apartment.
(because) She works from morning to night.

*C. Add words and ask questions. Answer them and add information.

EXAMPLE: a: **Do** you have a big family?
             b: No, I don't. I have only a mother and a sister.

1. __Do__ you have a big family?

2. Where __do__ your parents live? __do__ they work?

3. What __does__ your [father / (mother)] do? Where?

4. __do__ you have a [brother / (sister)] ?

5. How often __do__ you see [him / (her)] ?

6. What _do_ the people in your family like to do?

7. _do_ you write letters to your family?

8. _do_ they write to you? How often? Why (not)?

9. When _do_ you see your relatives? Where?

**D. Finish these questions about families. Answer them.

EXAMPLE: 1. **a:** Do you and your husband want more children?
            b: Yes, we do. We like large families.

1. Do _you have grandparents_ ?

2. Does _your brother have children_

3. Who _is married in your family_?

4. What _does your sister study_ ?

5. Where _do your parents live_ ?

6. When _do you go to Mexico_?

7. How often _do you go to the beach_?

8. Why _do you study English_?

Sasha			has	two sisters.	
His brother		usually	works		at night.
He			calls	him	once a week.
His wife	doesn't		like	to cook.	
She	doesn't		speak	English.	

**E. Tell or write about another student's family.

EXAMPLE: Sasha has a very big family, and many of his relatives live in this city. He sees his cousins once a week. They like to have big dinners in the city.

The Community

CHAPTER

6

COMPETENCIES:
Making and asking about plans
Making requests (at a bank, post office, restaurant, store, gas station)

GRAMMAR:
Be going to
Will/won't
Future time expressions
The verbs *take*, *get*, *do*, and *make*

83

PART ONE
Be Going to: Affirmative and Negative Statements

● Telling plans

We're going to go downtown.

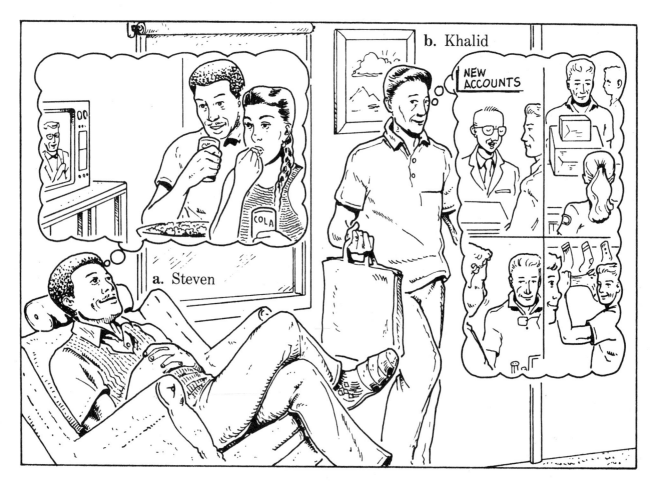

a. Steven

b. Khalid

a: My girlfriend is going to come over in the afternoon. We're going to watch the football game on T.V. How about you?

b: I'm going to go downtown.

a: Downtown? What for?

b: Well, first I have to go to the bank. I'm going to open a new account.

a: Really? Then can you please do me a favor? Can you deposit some checks for me?

b: Then I'm going to mail some packages at the post office.

a: The post office? Good. Then you can buy me a roll of stamps, O.K.?

b: Next I'm going to meet a friend for lunch. We're going to eat at the New World Restaurant.

a: Really? That's a terrific place. They have great desserts. My girlfriend loves them. Can you bring home an apple pie?

b: After lunch we're going to go shopping.

a: Shopping? Wonderful! Can you get me some socks?

What is the thing you like most about your family.

I	'm	going to	stay	home.
She	's	going to	bring	food.
My friends	are	going to	come	over.

The word *go* can be part of an expression.
Examples: We're going to **go** downtown. I'm going to **go** shopping.

A. Make sentences with these words. (Say or write them.)

EXAMPLE: 1. Joan: I'm going to spend the afternoon at Steven's house.

1. *I'm going to spend the afternoon at Steven house*
   spend the afternoon / I'm / at Steven's house / going to / .

2. *We're going to watch football on T.V.*
   going to / We're / watch football on T.V.

3. *I'm going to shopping for food*
   go shopping for food / I'm / going to / .

4. *Steven is going to make lunch*
   going to / Steven / make lunch / is / .

5. *We're going to eat all afternoon.*
   all afternoon / We're / going to / eat / .

B. Make sentences with these words.

EXAMPLE:
1. **Steven** is going to **get drinks**.   *He* [is / 's] going to _____ .
2. **Joan** is going to **buy food**.   _____ [is / 's] going to _____ .
3. **They're both** going to **eat all afternoon**.   They're both going to _____ .

Today's Plans

Steven:	1. get soft drinks	4. cook lunch	*7. (another plan)
Joan:	2. buy food	5. do the dishes	*8. (another plan)
Both:	3. eat all afternoon	6. watch football on T.V.	*9. (another plan)

| We | 're not | going to | stay | home. |
| They | aren't | going to | go | shopping. |

C. Make sentences with these words.

EXAMPLE: 1. I'm not going to go to school today.
I'm going to go downtown.

_____ not going to _____ today.
_____ going to _____ .

1.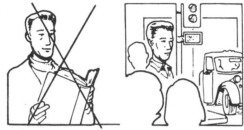

I'm / go to school
I'm / go downtown

2.

He's / withdraw money
He's / open a new account

3.

We're / bring lunch to the park
We're / eat in a restaurant

4.

He and his friend are / watch T.V.
They're / go shopping

5.

They're / drive
They're / take the bus

*6.

(sentences of your own)

*D.　Choose words and finish these sentences. You can use the pictures for ideas, but add information of your own, too.

EXAMPLES:　1. Today I'm going to apply for a driver's license.
　　　　　　2. I'm not going to take the driving test.

1. Today I'm going to _play basketball_____ .

2. I'm not going to _____ .

3. My family is going to _____ .

4. We aren't going to _____ .

5. My | husband / wife / brother / sister | is going to _____ .

6. He / She | isn't going to _____ .

7. My | parents / children / friends | are going to _____ .

8. They're not going to _____ .

**E.　Tell or write about the plans of another student and his or her family.

EXAMPLE:　Today Lorraine is going to go to the department of motor vehicles. She's going to apply for a driver's license.

PART TWO/ *Be Going to*: Questions and Answers

● Asking about Plans

What are you going to do today?

a: Khalid

b: Steven

a: What are you going to do today, Steven?

b: Joan and I are going to watch football on T.V.

a: Really? Listen, Steven, do you really plan to stay in all afternoon? When are you going to deposit your checks, buy stamps, and go shopping?

b: Tomorrow? The day after tomorrow? Next week? A month from now? In a year?

a: What's Joan going to say about your plans? Is she going to sit and eat with you all day? She's going to get sick! Aren't you going to get any exercise? How are you going to feel tonight? Why aren't you going to go out today?

b: You know, Khalid, you're right. I'm going to call her and change our plans. We're not going to watch T.V. at all. We're going to go downtown!

a: You are? Terrific! Then I don't need to go. I can stay home and watch the football game on T.V. Listen, Steve, can you do me some favors in the city?

| Are | you | going to | take | the bus? |
| Is | Joan | going to | bring | soft drinks? |

				he					we	
Yes,	I	am.	Yes,	she	is.		Yes,	you	are.
No,	I'm	not.		it				they	

	he's				he				we're				we	
No,	she's	not. = No,	she	isn't.		No,	you're	not. = No,	you	aren't.
	it's			it				they're				they	

A. Finish the questions and answers with these words. (Say or write them.)

EXAMPLE: 1. a: **Is** Steven **going to** wait for Joan at his house?
b: Yes, he **is**.

| Is | is | isn't | Are | are | aren't | going | to | not |

1. **Is** Steven **going** **to** wait for Joan at his house?   Yes, he **is**.

2. **Are** Steven and Joan **going** **to** walk to the bus stop?   Yes, they **are**.

3. **Are** they **going** **to** drive downtown?   No, they **aren't**.

4. **Are** they **going** **to** get off at State Street?   No, they're **not**.

5. **Is** Joan **going** **to** go with Steven to the bank?   No, she **isn't**.

Today's Plans

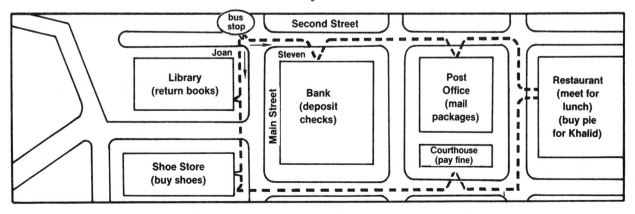

B. Finish these questions with *be going to*. Answer them with information from the map on page 89.

1. __Is__ Steven __going__ __to__ open an account at the bank?

2. __Is__ he __going__ __to__ buy stamps at the post office?

3. __Is__ Joan __going__ __to__ go to the library?

4. __Is__ she __going__ __to__ pay a fine at the courthouse?

5. __Are__ Steven and Joan __going__ __to__ meet for lunch?

6. __Are__ they __going__ __to__ go shopping after lunch?

*C. Ask and answer more questions with *be going to* about the plans on the map.

EXAMPLE: a: Is Joan **going to** go to the bank and the post office?
          b: No, she **isn't**. She's **going to** return books at the library and then buy shoes.

What	are	you	going to	do?	
Where	am	I	going to	eat?	
When	is	she	going to	leave?	
Why	aren't	they	going to	go	out?
How	are	we	going to	get	there?

D. Read the answers. Then finish the questions with *going to* and these words.

is	are	What	Where	When	Why

1. __What__ __is__ Steven __going__ __to__   Deposit checks.
do at the bank?

2. __Where__ __is__ he __going__ __to__   At the post office.
buy stamps?

3. __Why__ __is__ Joan __going__ __to__   Because she has to
go to the library?   return some books.

4. __When__ __are__ they __going__ __to__   At 1:00.
meet for lunch?

Who are you going to meet?   Who's going to meet you?

E. Read the answers. Then make questions with these words.

1. _Who's going to go to the bank and_ Steven.
   going to / Who's / go to the bank and post office / ? Post Office.

2. _Who's going to return book to the_ Joan.
   return books to the library / going to / Who's / ? library

3. _Who is she going to meet at the_ Steven.
   she / meet at the restaurant / is / Who / going to / ? restaurant.

4. _Who are they going to buy a_ Khalid.
   buy a pie for / going to / they / are / Who / ? pie for.

F. Ask questions for these answers. Don't include the underlined words.

EXAMPLE: 1. a: What are you going to do this morning?
             b: I'm going to study and then do housework.

1. _What are you going to do this morning_ ?
   I'm going to **study and then do housework.**

2. _Are you going to watch a T.V. movie_ ?
   Yes, I am. I'm going to watch a T.V. movie.

3. _Who are you going to meet_ ?
   I'm going to meet **some friends from work.**

4. _Where are you going to go_ ?
   We're going to go to **a shopping center.**

5. _What time are you going to leave_ ?
   We're going to leave **about 7:00.**

6. _Where are you going to eat_ ?
   We're going to eat **at the Good Earth Restaurant.**

7. _Where are you going_ ?
   We're going to drive.

8. _Who is going to pay._ ?
   We're all going to pay.

*Now answer the above questions with information about you.

When are you going to _____ ?				
tonight	next week	in an hour	=	an hour from now
tomorrow	next Monday	in a week	=	a week from now
the day after	next weekend	in two years	=	two years from now
tomorrow	next year	soon		someday

*G.   Make questions with these words. Answer them.

EXAMPLE: a: When is your girlfriend going to call you?
b: At about 8:00—in two hours.

When	are is	you your parents your child(ren) your friend(s) your classmate(s) _____ (s)	going to	come over? visit [you / your] _____(s)? call [you / your] _____(s)? get some exercise? go out (to _____)? _____ ?

*H.   Choose words and use words of your own. Ask and answer questions about plans.

1. Are you going to stay home tonight? [Why? / Why not?]

2. What are you going to do tomorrow? When? Where?

3. What is your [husband / wife / boyfriend / girlfriend / sister / brother / _____] going to do? When? Where? Why?

4. Are you going to go out on the weekend?

5. Who's going to go with you?

6. Where are you going to go?

7. How are you going to get there?

8. [Is / Are] _____ going to _____ ?

9. [What / Where / When / How] [is / are] _____ going to _____ ?

10. [Who's / What's] going to _____ ?

11. Why [isn't / aren't] _____ going to _____ ?

PART THREE   *Will/Won't*: Statements, Questions, and Answers

● Making Requests (at a Bank, Post Office, Restaurant, Store, Gas Station)

Will you please sign these checks?

The bus	will	be	late.		I'll	=	I will
I	'll	use	my credit card.		we'll	=	we will
He	'll	buy	a pie for dessert.		he	=	he will
We	'll	eat	at noon.		she'll	=	she will
					you'll	=	you will
					they'll	=	they will

A. Finish the sentences with *will* or *'ll* and these words. (Say or write them.)

EXAMPLE: 1. First we**'ll** take the bus downtown.

| stop | take | deposit | be | buy | walk |

First we <u>will take</u> the bus downtown. It <u>will stop</u> at the corner of
1.   2.

Second and Main. We can get off the bus there. We <u>will walk</u> two blocks to the
3.

bank. I <u>'ll deposit</u> these checks in my account. Then it <u>'ll be</u>
4.   5.

lunchtime. I <u>'ll buy</u> a pie for my roommate at the restaurant.
6.

| The checks | won't | clear | for a week. | | won't = will not |
| I | won't | drive | downtown. | | |

B. Finish the sentences with *won't* and these words.

EXAMPLE: 1. But the bus **won't stop** there.

| stop | pay | write | have |

The bank is on Second Avenue and Flower Street. But the bus <u>'ll stop</u> there.
1.

We'll have to walk two blocks. I <u>'ll pay</u> cash at the stores. I <u>'ll write</u>
2.   3.

checks. I'll use my credit card. And we <u>'ll have</u> lunch in an expensive restaurant.
4.

Will	you	sign	this?	Yes, of course. / Yes, I will.
Will	they	take	checks?	Sure. / No, they won't.
When will	they	clear?		

C. Finish the sentences with *will* or *won't* and these words.

EXAMPLES: 1. a: **Will** you **sign** here, please?
b: Yes, of course I **will**.

sign	clear

1.

a: <u>Will</u> you <u>sign</u> here, please?

b: Yes, of course I <u>will</u> .

When will the checks <u>clear</u> ?

a: In about five days.

take	show

2.

a: How can I help you?

b: <u>Will</u> you <u>take</u> a check?

a: <u>will</u> you <u>show</u> me some

identification, please?

b: Sure. Is a passport O.K.?

a: Yes, it is.

have	bring

3.

a: <u>Will</u> you <u>have</u> dessert?

b: Yes, thank you, we <u>will</u> .

<u>Will</u> you please <u>bring</u>

us the menus again?

a: Sure. Just a minute.

be	be

4.

a: <u>Will</u> this <u>be</u> all?

b: Yes, it <u>will</u> , thank you.

a: <u>Will</u> this <u>be</u> charge?

b: No, it <u>won't</u> .

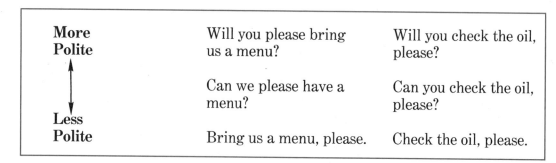

More Polite	Will you please bring us a menu?	Will you check the oil, please?
↕	Can we please have a menu?	Can you check the oil, please?
Less Polite	Bring us a menu, please.	Check the oil, please.

D. Finish the sentences with these words.

Can	Will	you	I	we

1. ___Can___ we please have some water?

2. ___Can___ you fill it up with gas, please?

3. ___Can___ I buy three rolls of stamps, please?

4. ___Can___ you please endorse these checks on the back?

5. ___Can___ ___I___ pay the bill with a credit card or a check?

6. ___Can___ ___you___ give me a receipt for the postage?

7. ___Can___ ___we___ please check the oil and clean the windshield?

8. ___Can___ ___you___ please fill out a deposit slip?

E. Now write the numbers of the above sentences in the boxes.

1.   2.   3.   4.

*F. Have conversations for the above pictures.

EXAMPLE: 1. a: What can I do for you?
                 b: Fill it up, please. And will you check the oil?

PART FOUR

The Verbs *Have*, *Take*, *Get*, *Do*, and *Make*; Review

- Making Plans

have = own or possess	take = carry or use	get = receive or buy
have | money a car _____	take | food with you (not eat) the car _____	get | a job some food _____
have = eat or drink	take = accept	get = go or arrive
have | breakfast lunch dinner coffee _____	take | a check there a credit card an order _____	get | to school back _____
	take = go on	get = become
have = experience	take | a bus a plane a trip _____	get | tired sick _____
have | a good time fun (free) time a party _____	take = have	
	take | a class a break _____	

A. Finish the sentences with these words.

| have   take   get |

EXAMPLE: **1.** Let's **have** a party.

Let's ___have___ a party! We can ___have___ dinner together. We'll ___get___
   1.   **2.**   **3.**

food at the market. I don't ___have___ any more cash. Will they ___take___ a check?
       4.   **5.**

How will we ___get___ there? Are we going to ___have___ the car?
    6.   **7.**

do	(house)work the dishes a favor _____	make	dinner a living noise _____

B. **Finish the sentences with these words.**

do	make

Who's going to ___do___ the work? Steven and I will ___make___ dinner.
         1.   **2.**

Can you ___do___ us a favor? Can you please ___make___ the salad? We'll all
      3.   **4.**

___do___ the dishes later.
5.

*C. **Finish the questions with these words. Answer them.**

EXAMPLE: **1.** **a:** When are you going to take a break from school?
             b: (I'm going to take a break) two months from now.

have	take	get	do	make

1. When are you going to ___take___ a break from school?

2. Are you going to ___take___ a trip? Where?

3. How will you ___get___ there? Will you ___get___ [a bus / a plane / your car] ?

4. When are you going to ___get___ back?

5. Where will you ___have___ [breakfast / lunch / dinner] tomorrow?

   What will you probably ___do___ ?

6. Are you going to ___have___ a party soon?

7. What food will you ___get___ from the store?

8. Who's going to ___do___ the work? Who will ___make___ dinner

   and ___do___ the dishes?

9. How do you ___take___ your living? Are you going to ___get___ a (different) job in the future?

We	're	going to	go	downtown next week.
Anita	isn't	going to	drive.	
The bus	will		stop	at the corner.
This store	won't		take	a check.

	Am	I	going to	pay?	No, you're not.
When	is	the bus	going to	come?	At 2:35.
Why	aren't	we	going to	drive?	It's too expensive.
	Will	you		help?	Yes, I will.
Where	will	Khalid		be?	Downtown.

D.

Make *going to* or *will* (*'ll*) sentences with similar meanings. Change the underlined words.

EXAMPLE: 1. a: We'll **go** to the bank. =
         b: We**'re going to go** to the bank.

1. We'll **go** to the bank. = _We're going to go to the bank_

2. I'm **going to cash** my paycheck. = _I'll cash my paycheck_

3. **Will** we **have** time for lunch? = _Where are you going to have time for lunch._

4. **Are** we **going to eat** out? = _I'll go to eat out._

5. Sure we **are**. = _Sure we will_

6. We**'re going to go** shopping on Main Street. = _We will go to shopping on Main Street._

7. I'll **buy** some new clothes. = _I'm going to buy some new clothes_

8. Where **will** we **park**? = _Where are we going?_

9. How **are** you **going to find** a place on the street? = _How you'll find a place on the street._

**E.

Tell about your future plans. Ask and answer questions. (You can work in small groups.)

EXAMPLE: a: Are you going to take more English classes?
         b: Yes, I am.
         c: What are you going to do this weekend?
         d: (We're going to) stay home and relax.

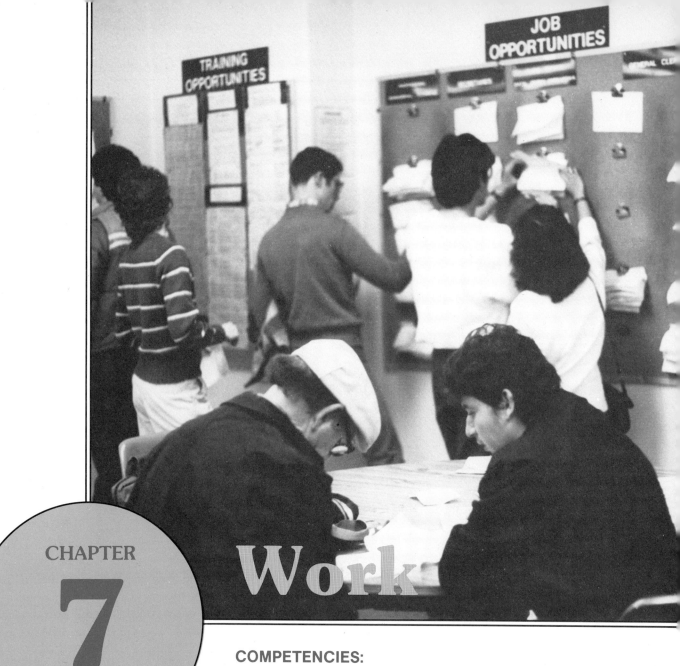

Work

COMPETENCIES:
Knowing ways to find work
Telling about work experience
Describing the day's work
Answering interview questions
Comparing jobs
Filling out job applications

GRAMMAR:
The simple past
Comparative forms
Reflexive pronouns

PART ONE
The Simple Past: Regular Verbs
(Affirmative and Negative Statements)

● Knowing Ways to Find Work ● Telling about Work Experience

He needed a job.

he learned about employment from
the job counselor at school.

He visited the state employment office
and filled out forms.

He talked to friends, classmates,
and relatives.

He studied the classified ads in the newspaper
and called some companies.

He walked around business areas of his city
and looked for "Help Wanted" signs.

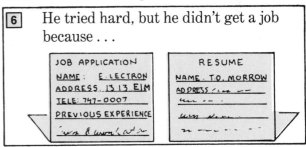

he didn't fill out applications neatly
or write a resume.

He didn't take any skills classes or
go to vocational school.

He didn't learn interview skills.

| I | wanted | a job. | My brother | helped | me. |
| We | typed | resumes. | He | | studied | the ads. |

A. Make past sentences with these words. (Say or write them.)

EXAMPLE: 1. Tran <u>want</u>ed <u>to buy a car</u>.
He <u>need</u>ed <u>a new job</u>.

1. Tran

want to buy a car
need a new job

2. He

talk to friends
listen to relatives

3. He

walk around the city
look for signs

4. Tran's sister

enroll in a class
learn about machines

5. She

use the library
study job information

6. She

visit an agency
fill out forms

7. his cousins

type resumes

8. They

look at job ads

9. They

call companies

I didn't cook.	He didn't wash dishes.	didn't = did not

B. Make sentences with the opposite meaning.

EXAMPLE: 1. **a:** I fixed cars.
          b: She **didn't fix** cars.

In my last job, I was a mechanic.	In her last job, Tran's sister was a secretary.
1. I **fixed** cars.	She _didn't fix cars_.
2. I **used** tools.	She _didn't use tools_.
3. I **changed** oil.	She _didn't change oil_.
4. I **worked** on engines.	She _didn't work on engines._
5. I **didn't answer** the phone.	She _I answered the phone_.
6. I **didn't talk** to customers.	She _I talked to customers_
7. I **didn't mail** packages.	She _I mailed packages._
8. I **didn't order** things.	She _I ordered things._

C. Make sentences about the pictures with these words and words of your own.

EXAMPLE: 1. In his last job, he managed a store.

In	her his their	last job(s),	he she they	(didn't)	type(d) and file(d). translate(d) letters. manage(d) a store. talk(ed) to customers. wash(ed) dishes. cook(ed) and clean(ed). _____ .

1.

2.

3.

must

D. Add sentences with these words and words of your own.

EXAMPLE: 1. In her last job, my sister was a bilingual secretary.
She answered the phone. She typed and filed.

answer the phone   play music   cook and clean
type and file   entertain people   wash dishes and clothes
translate letters   park cars   pack and carry boxes
manage apartments   prepare baby food   move furniture
clean carpets   change diapers
call repairpeople   watch T.V.

Let me see

1. In her last job, my sister was a bilingual secretary. _____
    She answered the phone. She typed and filed

2. My brother was an apartment manager. *He managed apartments,*
    cleaned carpets and called repair people

3. My aunt was a musician. *She entertained people*

4. My uncle was a parking lot attendant. *He packed and carried boxes.*

5. My son was a babysitter. *He prepared baby food*

6. My mother was a housewife. *She cooked and cleaned.*
    She washed dishes and clothes.

7. My cousins were movers. *They moved furniture*

*E. Choose words and finish these sentences.

EXAMPLE: 1. In my last job, I was a cashier. I cashed checks and counted money.

1. In my last job, I was a *cashier* . I *cash* ed
    checks and *count* ed *money* .

2. In [his / her] last job, my [father / mother / husband / wife] was a
    _____ . [He / She] _____ ed _____
    and _____ ed _____ .

PART TWO / The Simple Past: Irregular Verbs

● Describing the Day's Work

I did a lot today.

a. Bui

b. Yong

a: I'm tired.

b: You are? Why? What did you do today?

a: Well, I took care of the children. I read them stories and drew pictures for them. I taught them things. Their friends came over. They weren't tired, so they didn't sleep at all. Then I cooked and cleaned. The house was a mess. I did laundry. I wrote letters, and I paid bills. I ran around the block. I drove downtown. I went to the bank and the post office. I bought food, and I made a cake.

b: Well, of course you're tired! Why did you run around the block?

I	was	a teacher.	My sons	were	machinists.
She	wasn't	employed.	They	weren't	mechanics.

wasn't = was not   weren't = were not

A. Make sentences with the opposite meaning. (Say or write them.)

EXAMPLE: 1. a: Today **wasn't** a busy day.   b: Today **was** a busy day.

1. Today **wasn't** a busy day.   Today was a busy day.

2. There **weren't** many customers.   There were many customers.

3. There **weren't** a lot of problems.   There were a lot of problems.

4. The boss **wasn't** home sick.   The boss was home sick.

5. The other employees **were** there.   The other employees weren't there.

6. The secretary **was** at work.   The secretary wasn't at work.

7. The boxes **were** unpacked.   The boxes weren't unpacked.

8. I **was** bored.   I wasn't bored.

*B. Choose words and finish these sentences.

EXAMPLE: 1. Today there was an accident at work.

1. [(Yesterday) / Today] there [(was(n't)) / were(n't)] [a / (an) / some / any]
   accident at [home / work / (school)] .

2. The [neighbor / boss / secretary / other employees / (teacher)]
   [was(n't) / were(n't)] there .

| | I | keep | house. | | My wife | has | a job. |
| | I | kept | house. | | My wife | had | a job. |

	Same Form				**Consonant Changes**	
Present	cut	put	set		have	make
Past	cut	put	set		had	made

Vowel Changes						
Present	draw	drive	eat	get	give	read
Past	drew	drove	ate	got	gave	read
Present	run	sit	speak	take	write	
Past	ran	sat	spoke	took	wrote	

Vowel and Consonant Changes						
Present	bring	buy	do	go	keep	sell	tell
Past	brought	bought	did	went	kept	sold	told

For a list of irregular past forms, see page 169.

C. Finish these sentences with the correct forms of the words. (Say or write them.)

EXAMPLES: 1/2/3. We **spoke** and **read** and **wrote** English.

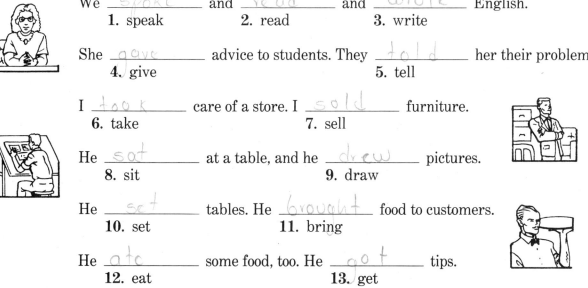

What did [you / he / she / they] do today?

We ___spoke___ and ___read___ and ___wrote___ English.
　　　1. speak　　　　**2.** read　　　　**3.** write

She ___gave___ advice to students. They ___told___ her their problems.
　　　4. give　　　　　　　　　　　**5.** tell

I ___took___ care of a store. I ___sold___ furniture.
　6. take　　　　　　　**7.** sell

He ___sat___ at a table, and he ___drew___ pictures.
　　8. sit　　　　　　　　　　**9.** draw

He ___set___ tables. He ___brought___ food to customers.
　　10. set　　　　　**11.** bring

He ___ate___ some food, too. He ___got___ tips.
　　12. eat　　　　　　　　　**13.** get

	Regular Past			Irregular Past		
cash	shave	try	cut	make	sell	buy
cashed	shaved	tried	cut	made	sold	bought

D. Make past sentences about the pictures with these words and words of your own.

EXAMPLE: 1. The bookkeeper **kept books and worked with numbers**.

keep books	cut hair	do laundry	drive around
work with numbers	shave beards	make beds	the city
cash checks	run machines	carry luggage	buy and sell
give out money	take orders	get tips	houses

1. The bookkeeper _Kept books and worked with numbers_.

2. The bank teller _Cashed checks and gave out money_ .

3. The barber _cut hair and shaved beards_ .

4. The machinist _ran machines and took orders_ .

5. The housekeeper _did laundry and made beds_ .

6. The bellhop _carried luggage and got tips_ .

7. The real estate agent _drove around the city and bought_ .
   and sold houses.

*8. I _got on the bus in the morning and went to_ .
   my first class

*E. Choose words and finish these past sentences with information about you and your classmates.

1. [Yesterday / Today] at [home / work / school / _____] , I

   (didn't) _____ (-ed) _____ .

2. _____ (name) _____ (didn't) _____ (-e)d

   _____ .

PART THREE   ## The Simple Past: Questions and Answers

● Answering Interview Questions

Tran has a job interview.

Was	the salary	good?	Yes, it was.
Were	your grades	high?	No, they weren't.
Did	you	have a job before?	Yes, I did.
Did	they	fire you?	No, they didn't.

A. Finish the questions with these words. Finish the answers. (Say or write them.)

EXAMPLE: **1. a:** Did you go to school in this country?   **b:** No, I didn't.

Did	Was	Were

1. _Did_ you go to school in this country?   No, _I didn't_ .

2. _Did_ you finish high school?   Yes, _I did._ .

3. _Was_ your first job in a bank?   No, _it wasn't_. It was in a post office.

4. _Were_ you happy with it?   Yes, _I, was_ .

Did	Were	go	take	learn

5. _Did_ you _go_ to vocational school?   No, _I, didn't._ .

6. _Did_ you _take_ business classes in high school?   Yes, _I did_ .

7. _were_ your grades good?   Yes, _they were._ .

8. _Did_ you _learn_ Spanish?   Yes, _I did._ .

Did	Does	Was	Were

9. _Were_ you good at math in high school?   Yes, _I was._ .

10. _Does_ your brother work at our bank now?   No, _he doesn't._ .

11. _Did_ he work here before?   Yes, _he did._ .

12. _Was_ he a teller then?   No, _he wasn't_ . He was a guard.

B. Ask questions for these answers.

EXAMPLES: 1. a: Did you graduate from high school in this country?
           b: No, I didn't. I graduated in my country.

1. _Did you graduate from high school in thi country?_
   No, I didn't. I graduated in my country.

2. _Did you take a lot of math classes?_
   Yes, I did. I took a lot of math classes.

3. _Were you good in language?_
   Yes, I was. I was very good at languages.

4. _Are you working now?_
   No, I'm not employed now.

5. _Do you like to work with money?_
   Yes, I do. I like to work with money.

Who	was			your supervisor?
What	were			your hours?
Where	did	you	work?	
How	did	they	get	to work?
When	did	she	leave	that job?

C. Make questions with these words. Answer them with information from the part of a job application form on the next page.

EXAMPLE: 1. a: Where did you go to elementary school?
          b: (I went to) Cat Linh School in Vietnam.

1. _Where did you go to elementary school?_
   did / you / Where / to elementary school / go / ?

2. _When did you graduate from high school?_
   graduate from high school / you / did / When / ?

3. _What was the name of your vocation school?_
   What / the name of your vocational school / was / ?

4. _What subjects did you study?_
   you / What subjects / did / study / ?

Education	Name of School	Dates	Did you graduate?	Main Subjects
Grammar School	Cat Linh Elementary School	1966-1970	yes	
High School	Dai La High School	1970-1974	yes	
College	Green Valley Community College	1982-1984	no	business
Business or Vocational School	Blaine Technical Institute	1986		electronics

D. Read the answers. Then finish the questions with these words.

What	When	Where	Did	did	were

1. _When_ _did_ you finish elementary school?   In 1978.

2. _Where_ _did_ you go to high school?   In my country.

3. _What_ _were_ your best subjects?   Math and science.

4. _Did_ you take college classes?   Yes, I did.

Who	Why	How	Were	was	did	didn't

5. _Why_ _didn't_ you graduate?   Because we moved.

6. _How_ _did_ you learn English?   I took a class at a local school.

7. _Who_ _was_ your teacher?   Mr. Howard.

8. _Were_ you a good student?   Yes, I was.

*E. **Make questions with these words and words of your own. Answer them with information from this part of a job application form.**

Who	is are was were	your	[present / last] job title? duties in your [present / last] job? [present / last] [boss / supervisor] ? salary per week / wages per hour? reason for leaving? _____ ?
What			

What Where When How much Why	do did	you	do in your [present / last] job? work? get a promotion? earn / make? leave? _____ ?
_____			

Work Experience	Name of Company	Job Title and Duties	Supervisor or Boss	Salary	Reason for Leaving
Present	Giant Burger	assistant manager	Ms. N Caserta	$6.00/ hour	
Past	Chu Wu Café	waiter	Mr. Tak Lee	$3.75/ hour	moved

When did you last _____ ?

today	last week	a week ago
yesterday	last Tuesday	two years ago
the day before yesterday	last year	a [short / long] time ago
	last _____	_____ ago

---

*F. **Make questions with these words and words of your own. Answer them with information of your own.**

EXAMPLE: a: When did you last apply for a job?
b: (I last applied for a job) six months ago.

When did you last	apply for a job? go to an interview? get [a promotion / a raise in salary] ? work / have a job? _____ ?

**G.   Answer these questions: How did you get your last job? What did you do to get it? (Examples: look in the classified ads, talk to friends, go to an employment agency.) You can work in small groups.

*H.   Ask questions with these words and words of your own. Answer them.

Did
Do
| you
> go to [school / college] in this country?
> finish [elementary / high / vocational] school / _____ ?
> take [English / math / business / typing] courses?
> [work / have a job] [now / before] ?
> type / have computer skills / know other languages?
> _____ ?

Are
> you employed (now)?
> you good at [languages / math / _____] ?
> _____ ?

Who
What
| is / are
was / were
| your
> boss / supervisor / _____ ?
> job title / duties / salary / _____ ?
> reason(s) for leaving your (last) job?
> _____ ?

What did you [study / do / _____] [before / last year / _____] ?

Where did you [go to school / learn English / work / _____] ?

When did you [graduate / change jobs / get a raise / _____] ?

Why did(n't) you [get a promotion / leave / _____] ?

PART FOUR
Comparative Forms; Reflexive Pronouns; Review of the Present, Past, and Future

● Comparing Jobs ● Filling out Job Applications

> In my last job,
>
> | the | boss | was | nice. | I | wanted | a | high | salary. |
> | He | paid | me | well. | We | worked | | long | hours. |
>
> In my new job,
>
> | the | boss | is | nicer. | I | want | a | higher | salary. |
> | He | pays | me | better. | We | work | | longer | hours. |
>
> | nice | busy | long | many | good / well |
> | nicer | busier | longer | more | better |
>
> | big | friendly | quiet | few | bad |
> | bigger | friendlier | quieter | fewer | worse |

A. Read. Then finish these sentences with the correct forms of the words. (Say or write them.)

EXAMPLE: 1. The coffee shop is **bigger**.
2. I can get **higher** pay.

You have a choice of two jobs. Which job are you going to take?

I'm not sure. Let me see.

The coffee shop is ___bigger___ .
     1. big

I can get ___higher___ pay.
     2. high

There are ___more___ employees.
     3. many

The boss is ___busier___ .
     4. busy

The food is ___better___ .
     5. good

The hours are ___shorter___ .
     6. short

The doughnut shop is ___smaller___ .
     7. small

The pay is ___lower___ .
     8. low

There are ___fewer___ employees.
     9. few

The boss is ___friendlier___ .
     10. friendly

The food is ___worse___ .
     11. bad

I'll have to work ___longer___ hours.
     12. long

> The work   is   more interesting.   It's   a   more important job.
>
> For short words, add -(e)r. For long words, use *more*.
> **Examples:** The place is noisier and more expensive.
> The work is harder and more boring.

B.

Finish these sentences with the correct forms of the words.

EXAMPLES: **1.** The coffee shop is **more comfortable**.

The coffee shop is _more comfortabl_   The doughnut shop is _newer_ .
1. comfortable   6. new

The work is _more interesting_ .   The work is _more boring_ .
2. interesting   7. boring

It's a _harder_ job.   It's an _easier_ job.
3. hard   8. easy

They serve _more expensive_ food.   I'll sell _cheaper_ food.
4. expensive   9. cheap

The place is _noisier_ .   The job title is _more important_ .
5. noisy   10. important

C.

Compare these jobs with forms of these words and words of your own. Make sentences with -(e)r and *more*.

EXAMPLE: I work **longer** hours in my present job. My position is **more important**.

| high | short | many | clean | easy | beautiful | important |
| low | long | few | dirty | hard | comfortable | expensive |

Work Experience				
	Title/duties	Hours	Salary/wages	Reason for leaving
Present Job Ann's Flower Shop	shop manager (supervise employees, order flowers)	8 a.m – 6 p.m. 5 days/week	$480/week	
Past Job Jan. '84 to Apr. '87 The Flower Box	salesclerk (sold flowers to customers)	6 hrs./day 3 days/week	$5.60/hour	I wanted a promotion and more responsibility.

*D. **Choose words and finish these sentences about two of your jobs.**

1. My present job is _____ *easi* er, and it's more _____ *interesting*.

   The pay is _____ *high* er, and my boss is _____ *more friendlier*.

2. My past job was _____ *cheap* er and more _____ *difficult*.

   Also, _____ .

| I worked for myself. | We can help ourselves. |
| He stayed by himself. | They enjoyed themselves. |

| myself | yourself | himself | themselves |
| ourselves | yourselves | herself | |

by oneself = alone

E. **Finish the sentences with these words.**

EXAMPLE: 1. I was in business for **myself**.

What did you do in your last job?

| I | me | myself |

I was in business for _____ *myself* . _____ *I* ran a small shop by _____ *myself* .
    1.   2.   3.

My relatives sometimes helped _____ *me* .
    4.

| She | her | herself |

My wife worked alone. _____ *She* was usually by _____ *herself* . Her employer was
    5.   6.

Ms. Johnson. My wife liked _____ *her* .
    7.

They	them	themselves

My children's supervisors were Mr. and Mrs. Sweet. __They__ worked for __themselves__
8.

in their store. __They__ often helped __themselve__ to the ice cream.
10.   11.

he	him	himself

My brother-in-law had a job far away from the city. He had to take care of __him__ , and
12.

__He__ sometimes talked to __himself__ . It was a good job for __him__ .
13.   14.   15.

We	we	us	ourselves

__We__ bought __us__ a computer. Customers brought work to __ourselves__
16.   17.   18.

and __we__ did it at home. We enjoyed __ourselves__.
19.   20.

you	yourself	yourselves

Did __you__ start a business by __yourself__ or did your husband help __you__ ?
21.   22.   23.

Did you two do well for __yourselves__ ?
24.

Past	My family		worked	very hard.
	We		had	a delivery truck.
	My wife		was	in business for herself.
	I	didn't	take	care of myself.
Present	My brother		is	a post office employee.
	He		manages	a bigger department now.
	They		pay	him better.
	I	don't	answer	the telephone.
	My employer	doesn't	keep	the books well.

*F. First, fill out this job application for youself. Then make sentences about the information.

EXAMPLE: I started Grant Elementary School in New York in 1974 and left in 1980. I graduated from Lincoln High School in 1986. I studied machine shop there.

JOB APPLICATION				
Education	Name and Location of School	Dates	Did you graduate?	Subjects Studied
Elementary School	Grant Elementary School in New York	1974 to 1980		
High School		1986	Yes	
College Business/ Vocational School				

Past Employers (Start with the last job first.)

Date	Name and Location	Salary	Position	Reason for Leaving
from to				
from to				
from to				

	Did	you	graduate	from high school?	Yes, I did.
	Were	you	a good student?		No, I wasn't.
What	did	you	do	in your last job?	I cooked.
When	did	you	leave	it?	A month ago.
How	was			your salary?	Very good.
	Do	you	need	higher pay?	Yes, I do.
	Are	you		bilingual?	Yes, I am.
Who	is	your		boss?	Ms. Jackson.
Where	do	you	work	now?	At a hospital.
Why	do	you	want	to change jobs?	I want more responsibility.

*G. Ask and answer questions about the job application on this page.

EXAMPLES: a: Where did you go to elementary school?
b: I went to Grant School in New York from 1974 to 1980.

CHAPTER 8

Shopping

COMPETENCIES:
Expressing likes and dislikes
Making requests and getting help
Asking for and giving permission
Telling possibilities
Reading labels on clothing
Giving advice
Making comparisons
Reading store ads

GRAMMAR:
Modal verbs
Indefinite pronouns
Infinitives of purpose
Superlative forms

Modal Verbs of Desire, Request, and Permission; Indefinite Pronouns:
PART ONE　Questions and Answers

- Expressing Likes and Dislikes ● Making Requests and Getting Help
- Asking for and Giving Permission

Id' like some new shirts.

| I'd | like | | a blouse. | | My son | would like | | a shirt. |
| We'd | like | to go | shopping. | | He | 'd like | to buy | jeans. |

| I'd | = | I would | you'd | = | you would | he'd | = | he would |
| we'd | = | we would | they'd | = | they would | she'd | = | she would |

A. Make sentences with these words. (Say or write them.)

EXAMPLE: 1. **Joan** would like to **buy a blouse.**   _____ [would / 'd] like to _____ .
         She'd like **long sleeves.**   _____ 'd like _____ .

1.

Joan / buy a blouse
She / long sleeves

2.

We / see some slacks
We / something in blue

3.

Steven / try on shirts
He / a sweater, too

4.

I / buy you a coat
But you / that car

5.

They / have some money
They / a lot of toys

*6.

	Would	you	like		a bigger size?
	Would	he	like	to try	it on?
What color	would	they	like?		

B. Finish the questions with these words. Then find the answers.

EXAMPLE: 1. a: **Would** you like short sleeves?
b: Yes, I would.

Do	do	want	Would	would	like

1. _Would_ you like short sleeves?   No, thank you.

2. _Do_ you want stripes?   How about blue?

3. What color _do_ you _want_ ?   Yes, I would.

4. What size _do_ you _like_ ?   I'd like cotton.

5. What fabric _would_ you _like_ ?   I'll try on size 15.

C. Ask questions for these answers.

EXAMPLES: 1. What size would you like to try?   *or*   What size do you take?
What size? I wear a 36 long.

1. _What size would you like to try?_
What size? I wear a 36 long.

2. _What fabric would you like?_
What fabric? I'd like wool.

3. _Would you like pants with pockets?_
Yes, please. I'd like pockets.

4. _____
No, thanks. I don't want stripes.

5. _Do you like_
Yes, I do. I like knits, too.

6. _____
What color? I'd like to try brown, please.

| May | I | look at some more styles? | Of course. All right. |
| Could | we | try on these slacks, please? | Sorry, but . . . |

D. Have conversations for the pictures with these words and words of your own.

EXAMPLE: 1. b: May I help you?
  a: Yes, please. Could I see some blouses in size 34?
  b: Of course. Would you like to try cotton?

Can	I			look at	some [blouses / slacks] ?
Could	we		(please)	see	a [larger / smaller] size?
May	she			try	something in [blue / red] ?
	___			try on	something in [wool / cotton] ?
				___	_____ ?

1.
2.
3.

| Could | you | wait on me, please? | Sure. All right. |
| Would | you | please show us some sweaters? | Sorry. I'm busy now. |

E. Have conversations for the above pictures with these words.

EXAMPLE: 1. a: Can you please wait on me?
  b: Of course. What would you like?
  a: Could you show me some blouses in more colors?

Can			[help / wait on] [me / us] ?
Could	you	(please)	show me some more [colors / styles] ?
Will			bring her a [smaller / bigger] size?
Would			_____ ?

Could	you	please help us?	**People**
Is this a gift for	a friend?		someone = somebody
I'd like to see	a shirt	in size 15, please.	
Could	someone	please help us?	**Things**
Is this a gift for	somebody	else?	something
I'd like to see	something	in size 15, please.	

F. Finish the sentences with these words.

someone	somebody	something

a: Could _somebody_ please help me? I'd like to see _____ in cotton.
    1.   **2.**

b: Of course. May I show you _____ with long sleeves? Is this for you, or is
                                3.

it a gift for _____ else? Would you like to try _____ in blue?
            4.   **5.**

Can	somebody / someone	help us?	We	want to buy	something.
Can't	anybody / anyone	help us?	We don't	want to buy	anything.

G. Finish the sentences with these words.

somebody / someone	anybody / anyone	something	anything

a: Can _____ wait on us? I don't see _____ in the women's clothing
        1.   **2.**

department. Where are all the clerks? Isn't there _____ on this floor?
                                                3.

b: I'd like _____ in cotton or wool. I don't like to buy _____ in
            4.   **5.**

polyester fabrics. Would you like _____ in green or yellow?
                                6.

*H. Choose words and finish the questions. Answer them.

EXAMPLES: 1. **a:** Would you like to go shopping for children's clothes?
  b: No, I wouldn't. I don't have children.
  a: Where would you like to shop?
  b: I'd like to go to a men's shop.

1. Would you like to go shopping for [men's / women's / children's] clothes?

2. Where would you like to shop?

3. Would you like to go with [someone / somebody] ?

4. [Can / Could / May] I go with you?

5. [Can / Could / Would] you [drive / take the bus] with [me / _____] ?

6. What would you like to buy?

*I. Have conversations for the pictures with these words and words of your own.

EXAMPLE: **a:** I'd like to see some party dresses, please.
  b: Would you like to see something in a solid color?
  a: Yes, I would. Could I try pink or light blue?
  b: Of course. What size can I show you?

Would you like (to see)

Could I [see / look at] | something | in [brown / red / _____] ?
in [wool / polyester / _____] ?
with [long / short] sleeves?
with [stripes / a pattern] ?
in another [size / style / _____] ?

What | size
color(s)
style(s)
fabric | [can / could] I show you?
would you like to [see / look at / try] ?
would you like?

Modal Verbs of Possibility: Affirmative and Negative; **PART TWO** Infinitives after Nouns and Pronouns

● Telling Possibilities ● Reading Labels on Clothing

He might like a sweater.

a: Maybe I'll buy Steven a present today.

b: Oh? What would he like?

a: I'm not sure. Maybe he'd like something for parties. He might like a sweater.

b: How about this striped one?

a: It's nice, but he may not like the pattern. The colors might not go with his slacks, and they may fade.

b: That solid-colored brown one is beautiful.

a: Yes, it is, but it may be too warm for him. And he may not want to dry-clean it. He'll wash it by hand, and he'll twist and wring it. He may not dry it flat, and it will lose its shape.

b: How about that cotton turtleneck one?

a: It looks fine now, but he might wash it in hot water. It may shrink. He might put it in the dryer instead of on the line. And it will need ironing.

b: Look at this one.

a: Maybe I won't buy Steven a present today. Let's get some food.

Maybe	he'd		like	a	sweater.	Maybe	it	will	fade.
He	may	like	a	sweater.		It	may	fade.	
He	might	need	a	tie.		It	might	shrink.	

A. Make two sentences with the same meanings. (Say or write them.)

EXAMPLES: 1. a: **Maybe I'll get** Steven a jacket. =

              b: **I may get** Steven a jacket.   *or*   **I might get** Steven a jacket.

1. **Maybe I'll get** Steven a jacket. = _____

2. **Maybe he wants** a new shirt. = _____

3. **Maybe he needs** jeans. = _____

4. **Maybe he wants** a tie. = _____

5. **Maybe I'll ask** him. = _____

He might like a blue	sweater.	I may buy	this.
He might like a blue	one.	I may buy	this one.

B. Look at the ad and make sentences about it with these words.

EXAMPLE: a: **My boyfriend** might like **a blue** one.   a: _____ might _____ one.

            b: **I** may **buy a long-sleeved** one.   b: _____ may _____ one.

            a: A **cotton** one might **be better**.   a: A _____ one might _____ .

Sale on Men's Sweaters

wool round neck

regular	**$43.95**	sale	**$35.95**

striped	black	white
patterned	grey	brown
solid colored	blue	green

cotton

	reg.	sale
long-sleeved	**$25.00**	$18.00
short-sleeved	**$16.00**	$12.00
	turtleneck	**V-neck**

| He | may | wash it. | He | may | not | dry-clean it. |
| It | might | shrink. | It | might | not | need ironing. |

C. Make sentences about the labels.

EXAMPLE: 1. He may not wash it by hand.
He may wash it in the machine.
And he might not dry it on the line.

1.
Hand wash
separately.
Line dry.

2.
Dry-clean only.
Do not iron.

3.
Do not twist or
wring. Reshape.
Dry it flat.

4.
Machine wash
cold. Do not
dry-clean.

| I | want | to buy | a dress. |
| We'd | like | to eat | something. |

| I | want | a dress | to wear to parties. |
| We'd | like | something | to eat. |

D. Make sentences with these words.

1. _____
I / to buy myself a dress / want / might / .

2. _____
something / may / need / I / to wear to a party / .

3. _____
Let's get / to drink / something / .

4. _____
to eat / Do you want / something / too / ?

5. _____
to go out / to a restaurant / like / I'd / .

*E. Make sentences or have conversations for the picture with these words and words of your own.

EXAMPLE: **a:** My sister would like a new dress.
             b: That yellow wool one might be nice.

I			dress(es).
My husband	'd		shirt(s).
My wife	would	like a	blouse(s).
My sister(s)	may	some	sweater(s).
My child(ren)	might		jacket(s).
My _____ (s)			_____ (s).
He / She / _____			

	polyester / cotton			be too warm.
The	patterned / striped			be nice.
This	red and white	one may	(not)	lose its shape.
That	bigger / smaller	might		shrink or fade.
	turtleneck / V-neck			need ironing.
	short-sleeved			need dry cleaning.
				_____ .

**F. Look at clothing ads in your local newspaper. Have conversations about them. (You can work in small groups.)

EXAMPLE: **a:** Would you like the outfit in the ad from Northstar's Department Store?
             b: No, I wouldn't. I'd like something in that style, but I couldn't wear those colors.

PART THREE

Modal Verbs of Advice (Statements and Questions); Infinitives of Purpose; More Indefinite Pronouns

● Giving Advice

To save money, you should look for bargains.

1. To save money you should always look for bargains. We ought to buy all our clothes at clearance sales. We shouldn't worry about the latest styles. To get good prices, I usually buy winter clothes at the end of the season.

END OF SEASON CLEARANCE SALE
All Prices Reduced
25%

2. We ought to buy some new sheets and towels now. There are white sales only twice a year. Should we get these? I'll charge everything on my account. We won't have to pay for them this month.

WHITE SALE
Everything ½ Price. Last Week!

SHEETS

3. Everyone will be at this store tomorrow. I have to get here early to get the best buys. I shouldn't forget my credit card. What should I buy?

ONE DAY SALE TOMORROW ONLY!
Prices Cut 20 to 50%
Great Bargains!

4. We sure saved a lot of money!

BILL
BILL
BILL

Yes	No
You have to charge it.	You don't have to pay cash.
We should get bargains.	We shouldn't pay too much.
I ought to look for sales.	
	shouldn't = should not

A. Make sentences with the opposite meanings. (Say or write them.)

EXAMPLE: 1. a: You **don't have to pay** cash at this store.   b: You **have to pay** cash at this store.

Brock Brothers   [signs: we accept all major credit cards. / ONE-DAY SALE ON MEN'S CLOTHING Saturday Only. / WHITE SALE BEGINS NEXT MONTH.]

Smith's Store   [signs: CA$H ONLY / WHITE SALE THIS WEEK ONLY]

1. You **don't have to pay** cash at this store.   _____

2. We **shouldn't get** sheets and towels now.   _____

3. I **have to bring** my credit card.   _____

4. I **should buy** myself a gift.   _____

B. Finish the sentences with these words. (There are many correct answers.) You may want to add words.

EXAMPLES: 1. In my opinion, we **shouldn't** try to save money all the time. But we **ought to** look for bargains.

(don't) have to   should(n't)   ought (not) to

In my opinion, we _____ try to save money all the time. But we _____
                        1.   2.

look for bargains. We _____ buy our clothes at clearance or end-of-season sales. We
                                  3.

_____ look for the latest styles. I believe you _____ pay cash for things most
4.   5.

of the time. You _____ use credit cards or open charge accounts.
                              6.

C. Make sentences with these words and words of your own.

EXAMPLE: To save money, you shouldn't use credit cards.

To save money,
To charge things,
To take care of clothing,
To choose the right sizes,
To open a charge account,
To buy presents,
To _____ ,

I	(don't) have to	look for bargains and discounts.
we	should(n't)	fill out an application form.
you	ought to	use credit cards.
		try on clothes.
		look at many styles.
		read the labels.
		_____ .

| I | might | buy | something. | My brother | wants | to buy | everything. |
| We | won't | get | anything. | He | can't | buy | everything. |

D. Finish the sentences with these words.

EXAMPLE: 1. Occasionally she might buy **something** for her children.

| something | anything | everything |

My sister doesn't like to shop for clothes. Occasionally she might buy _____ for
                                                                                    1.

her children, but she won't buy _____ for herself. She thinks _____ in the
                                            2.   **3.**

stores is too expensive, so she sews almost _____ for the family. My brother loves to
                                                          4.

shop at discount stores. Today he's going to buy _____ for himself and his family.
                                                              5.

He gets _____ on sale. He doesn't want to buy _____ at full price.
              6.   **7.**

	Should	I	charge	things or pay cash?
What	should	we	buy?	
Where	should	we	look	for sales?

E. Read the answers. Then finish the questions with these words.

EXAMPLE: a: **Where should** we go shopping?
b: At a shopping center.

What	Where	Should	should

1. _____ _____ we go shopping?   At a shopping center.

2. _____ we look in the yellow pages   We should look in the
first or just go there?   phone book first.

3. _____ stores _____ we call?   The furniture stores
and the fabric shops.

4. _____ _____ we find out about   In the newspaper.
sales?

F. Make questions from these words and words of your own. Answer them with your opinions.

EXAMPLE: a: Should I wash clothes by hand or by machine?
b: I think you should wash most things by machine.

Should	I we you	shop downtown or at shopping centers?
		look for sales or pay full prices?
		go to discount stores or department stores?
		wash clothes by hand or by machine?
		_____ ?

What			try to buy [on sale / at a discount / _____] ?
Where			shop for [clothes / furniture / toys / _____] ?
When	should	I we you	buy [winter / summer] clothes?
How			pay for things?
Why			_____ ?

**G. Look at ads for clothing stores in the telephone yellow pages. Answer these questions: Where do you think you ought to shop? How should you get there? What should you buy? (Work in small groups.)

PART FOUR / Superlative Forms; Review

● Making Comparisons ● Reading Store Ads

The blue shirt may be   the warmest   (of the three).

| large | pretty | much / many | good / well |
| largest | prettiest | most | best |

| big | long | little | bad |
| biggest | longest | least | worst |

 A. **Finish the sentences with the correct forms of these words. (Say or write them.)**

EXAMPLE: **1.** The cotton blouse has the **longest** sleeves.

Which of the three blouses should I buy?

The cotton blouse has the _____ sleeves. It may be the _____ and the
                         1. long   **2.** heavy

_____ , and it's the _____ size. It has the _____ fabric and the
3. warm   **4.** big   **5.** much

_____ decoration. The silk one might be the _____ and _____
6. little   **7.** light   **8.** cool

of the three. It has the _____ sleeves. The pattern looks the _____ and the
                        9. short   **10.** nice

decoration is the _____ . I think it's the _____ blouse. The polyester one
              11. pretty   **12.** good

is the _____ color. It's the _____ of all the blouses. It's the _____ .
    13. dark   **14.** cheap   **15.** small

I think it's the _____ one to buy, too.
          16. bad

> The wool coat is   the most expensive   (of all).

B. Make sentences about the three pictures on page 135. Use *the most*, these words, and words of your own.

EXAMPLE: The silk blouse is **the most delicate** of the three.

> delicate   beautiful   comfortable   expensive   practical

*C. Make sentences about the ads from the telephone yellow pages with these words and words of your own.

EXAMPLES: a: The **Clair Bargain Center** has the **low**est **prices** of the four stores.

_____ has the _____ est _____ of the four stores.

b: The **Big Man's Shop** has the most **clothing in large sizes**.

_____ has the most _____ .

Ads from the Yellow Pages

---**BIG MAN'S SHOP**---
Complete Selection to Size 54
Suits • Sport Coats • Slacks
Jackets • Shoes • Sweaters
Shirts • Work Clothes
Most Major Credit Cards
Free Parking
1069 Fairview   555-4480

JIMMY'S SMALL AND SHORT
Fine Clothing for
the Small and Short Man
Most Major Brands
We accept Mastercard and Visa.
16000 Oak Dr.   555-5433

BOB BROWN'S DESIGNER CLOTHING
FOR MEN
Mon. - Sat. 10 a.m. - 6 p.m.
12234 S. Main St.   **555-5645**
Low, low discount prices

CLAIR BARGAIN CENTER
Best Prices on the East Side
Large Selection of:
• *Used Furniture* • *Clothing*
• *Lamps* • *Tools*
• *Appliances* • *Shoes*
• *Housewares* • *Books*
• *Office Equipment* • *Toys*
DOLLAR A BAG CLOTHING SALES
Open Mon., Wed., Sat. 9-5
Donations Accepted.
Call 555-9000 for Pick-Up.

I'd like		to	get something to wear.
Men's shirts	may (not)		be on sale.
We	might not		want to buy anything.
You	ought	to	use credit cards.
Your husband	should(n't)		buy everything at one store.

To get the best buys,	you	(don't)	have	to	read labels.
To save money,	I	'll	buy		the cheapest one.

*D.   Make sentences about the ads on page 136 with these words.

EXAMPLES:

I'd like **to go to the Big Man's Shop**.

But they may not **have my size**.

Maybe I ought to **try the Clair Bargain Center**.

Prices should **be lower there**.

I'd like _____ .

_____ [may / might (not)]

_____ .

_____ ought to _____ .

_____ .

_____ should(n't) _____ .

	Would	you	like	to buy somebody a gift?
What color	would	you	like?	
	Could	I	help	you with something?
	May	we	try	on these slacks?
	Would	you	show	us some wool sweaters, please?
	Should	we	go	to a discount store?
Where	should	they	look	for bargains?

E.   Have conversations for these pictures.

EXAMPLE: a: Would you like to try on a larger size?
b: Yes, please. And could you show me something in brown?

CHAPTER

9

Health

COMPETENCIES:
Asking about and describing health habits
Filling out a medical information form
Describing past activities and events
Describing amounts

GRAMMAR:
The present and past continuous
Quantity expressions

The Present Continuous:
PART ONE — Affirmative and Negative Statements; Contrast with the Simple Present

● Describing Health Habits

I'm feeling terrific!

a: Maria

b: Anita

a: I'm feeling great today! Do you want to get together?

b: I'd love to, Maria, but I can't. I'm busy exercising right now.

a: Really? Then how about lunch?

b: Thanks, but I'm not having lunch today. I'm meeting Joan, and we're jogging in the park.

a: Oh? Well, would you like to meet for coffee and dessert in the afternoon?

b: Sorry, but we're not drinking coffee now. And I'm not eating any more sugar. I'm dieting.

a: I see. Then we could go to the supermarket together.

b: Well, we could, but we aren't buying supermarket food these days. At this moment, Joan is shopping at the health food store. She's getting things for dinner tonight.

a: Terrific! Then I'd like to invite you to a movie after that.

b: Thank you, but I have to get to bed early. I need a lot of sleep.

a: Wow! You're really taking care of your health! I bet you're feeling wonderful!

b: Not really, Maria. I'm feeling terrible. You see, I'm not having any fun!

I'm	feeling	sick.	We're	having	dinner.
Joan is	shopping	downtown.	You're	meeting	Anita.
She's	buying	food.	They're	waitiing	for you.

A. Finish these sentences with the correct forms of the words. Add necessary words. (Say or write them.)

Right now . . .

At this moment . . .

EXAMPLES: 1. Anita is **feeling** tired.

7. Maria and Edgar are **enjoying** this.

Anita is _____ tired.
1. feel

Maria and Edgar are _____ this.
7. enjoy

Anita is _____ T.V.
2. watch

Maria and Edgar are _____ .
8. eat

She's _____ .
3. exercise

They're _____ chicken.
9. have

Joan is _____ .
4. cook

Maria is _____ coffee.
10. drink

She's _____ dinner.
5. make

She's _____ good.
11. feel

They're _____ home
6. stay

Edgar is _____ the family
12. take

tonight.

to the movies tonight.

*B. Finish these sentences about you and people in your class.

EXAMPLE: 1. Right now I'm **thinking about lunch**.

1. Right now I'm _____ ing _____ .

2. _____ (name) is _____ ing _____ at this moment.

3. _____ (name) and _____ (name) _____ are _____ ing _____ .

I'm	not	feeling	tired.	We're	not	doing	anything.
He	isn't	exercising.		They	aren't	sleeping	enough.

we're (you're, they're) not = we (you, they) aren't
he's (she's) not = he (she) isn't

C. Finish the sentences with the opposite meanings.

EXAMPLE:
1. a: Anita and Joan **aren't eating** right now.
   b: Maria and Edgar **are eating** right now.

1. Anita and Joan **aren't eating** right now.

   Maria and Edgar _____ _____ .

2. They**'re not drinking** coffee.

   They _____ .

3. Anita **isn't enjoying** herself.

   Maria _____ .

4. Joan **is cooking**.

   Edgar _____ .

5. She's **making** a lot of food.

   He _____ .

6. Anita **is exercising**.

   Maria _____ .

7. She's **feeling** tired.

   She _____ .

8. Anita and Joan **are staying** home tonight.

   Maria and Edgar _____ _____ .

*D. Choose words and finish these sentences.

EXAMPLE: Tonight I'm **go**ing **out to dinner**. I'm not **cook**ing.

1. Tonight I'm _____ ing _____ . I'm not _____ ing _____ .

2. My [mother / husband / daughter / cousin / _____] is

   _____ ing _____ . [He / She] ['s not / isn't]

   _____ ing _____ .

3. My [parents / children / _____] are _____ ing _____ .

   They ['re not / aren't] _____ ing _____ .

All the Time	Right Now / In the Future
I exercise twice a week. We always eat well. My husband cooks every day.	I'm exercising right now. We're eating well tonight. He's cooking tomorrow.
never occasionally sometimes often usually always every [(two) day(s) / _____] once a week twice a month	(right) now at this moment these days today tonight this [afternoon / _____] tomorrow next [week / _____]

*E. Finish the sentences with the correct forms of these words. Add necessary words.

EXAMPLES: 1. You're **taking** care of yourself these days, right?
               4. Anita and I **exercise** three times a week.

a: You look great! You _____ care of yourself these
                          1. take

days, right? I see you _____ weight now.
                     2. gain

b: Yes, I _____ more these days. Anita and I _____
         3. eat   **4. exercise**

three times a week, and we don't usually _____ to school.
                                    5. drive

We _____ our bicycles every day. We _____ terrific!
     6. ride   **7. feel**

a: Anita _____ her weight now, too, right?
        8. watch

b: Yes, she is. She _____ today and _____ tonight.
         9. shop   **10. cook**

At this moment, she _____ in the park. She _____ to
             11. run   **12. go**

a health club several times a week. And she never _____ now.
                               13. smoke

*F. **Choose words and finish these sentences. You can use the pictures for ideas, but add information of your own, too.**

1. I'm (not) taking care of myself these days.

2. I'm feeling │ good / bad │ because I'm _____ .

3. I'm (not) │ gaining / losing │ weight because I'm (not) │ eating / drinking / smoking │ a lot.

4. My │ husband / wife / friend │ exercises / doesn't exercise │ a lot.
_____

5. We │ never / sometimes / usually │ walk / run / swim │ together. We _____ │ every evening. / every two days. / once a week.
_____   _____

6. Tonight / Tomorrow / Next week │ we're _____ .
_____

PART TWO   The Present Continuous: Questions and Answers

● Asking about Health Habits ● Filling out Medical Information Forms

Are you feeling all right now?

Questions, questions, questions! Did I have any of these diseases? Do I have a medical checkup every year or two? Who am I going to for dental care? How am I getting exercise? Am I gaining or losing weight? Am I a smoker? Are we paying attention to our diet? What foods are we eating? What medicine do I take? Who's paying my medical bills? Do I have insurance? When...? Where...? Why...?

Can I ask you something? What are you checking now? What's that thing measuring? How's my blood pressure?

Questions, questions, questions! Who...? What...? How...?

| Are | you | | getting | enough sleep these days? | Yes, I am. |
| Is | your | doctor | giving | you good advice? | No, he isn't. |

A. Finish the questions with these words. Answer them.

EXAMPLE: 1. a: <u>**Do**</u> you get regular medical checkups?
            b: <u>No</u>, I don't.

| Do | Does | Is | Are |

1. _____ you get regular medical checkups? _____

2. _____ you feeling healthy now? _____

3. _____ you usually eat and sleep well? _____

4. _____ you losing or gaining weight? _____

5. _____ your doctor give you advice? _____

6. _____ your insurance paying your bill? _____

B. Ask questions for these answers.

EXAMPLE: 1. a: Are you following a special diet now?
            b: No, I'm not. I'm not following a special diet.

1. _____
        No, I'm not. I'm not following a special diet.

2. _____
        No, he isn't. He's not giving me any medication.

3. _____
        Yes, we do. We exercise and eat good food every day.

4. _____
        No, I don't smoke.

5. _____
        Yes, I am. I'm taking good care of my teeth and my eyes.

How much rest	are	you	getting?
Where and when	is	she	exercising?
Why	isn't	your insurance	paying this bill?

C. Read the answers. Finish the questions with these words.

EXAMPLE: 1. a: __Where is__ Steven going on May 13?
            b: To the doctor.

APPOINTMENT

For Steven _____

M   T   W   T   F

on May 13 at 2:30 a.m. (p.m.)

Dr. Bass Medical Clinic for Headache
12364 Medical Center Dr. 555-2785

Who	What	Where	When	Why	is

1. _____ _____ Steven going on May 13?   To the doctor.

2. _____ _____ Steven visiting?   Dr. Bass.

3. _____ _____ he going?   At 2:30.

4. _____ _____ he going?   Because he's not feeling well.

5. _____ problems _____ he having?   Headaches.

Who's	paying the bill?	who's = who is
What's	going on?	what's = what is

D. Read the answers. Finish the questions with these words.

What's	Who's	what's	going	bothering	sending	paying

1. Well, Mr. Lasky, _____ _____ on?   I'm sick.

2. _____ _____ you?   My head and ears.

3. _____ _____ us your records?   Our family doctor.

4. _____ _____ your bill?   I am.

E. Ask a classmate questions with these words and words of your own. (You'll find more vocabulary on the medical information form.) Fill in the form with your classmate's answers.

Do you have [medical insurance / a family doctor / _____] ?
[headaches / backaches / earaches / _____] ?
problems with your [skin / heart / eyes / _____] ?
[allergies / high blood pressure / _____] ?
_____ ?

Do you | smoke?
drink alcohol?
take any drugs?
exercise?
_____ ?

Are you | eating well?
sleeping enough?
getting enough rest?
taking any medications?
_____ ?

Who
Where | are you | seeing
going | for | eye examinations?
dental care?
regular checkups?
_____ ?

What kinds of | medicines
exercise
food
activities
_____ | are you | taking?
doing?
eating?
enjoying?
_____ ?

Medical Information Form

1. Medical Insurance _____ Policy Number _____

2. Health problems? (Check *yes* or *no*).

problems with your:

	yes	no		yes	no		yes	no		yes	no
headaches	☐	☐	backaches	☐	☐	heart	☐	☐	nose	☐	☐
earaches	☐	☐	high blood			lungs	☐	☐	bones	☐	☐
sore throats	☐	☐	pressure	☐	☐	stomach	☐	☐	skin	☐	☐
many colds	☐	☐	other:			teeth	☐	☐	other:		
toothaches	☐	☐	_____	☐	☐	eyes	☐	☐	_____	☐	☐

3. Health habits? (Check *yes* or *no*).

	yes	no		
smoke	☐	☐	How often? _____	
drink alcohol	☐	☐	What? _____	How much? _____
take drugs	☐	☐	What? _____	How often? _____
exercise	☐	☐	What? _____	How often? _____
eat well	☐	☐	What foods? _____	
allergies	☐	☐	To what? _____	
medications	☐	☐	What? _____	How often? _____

Family doctor _____

Eye doctor _____ Dentist _____

PART THREE
The Past Continuous: Statements, Questions, and Answers

● Describing Past Activities and Events

What were you doing at the time of the earthquake?

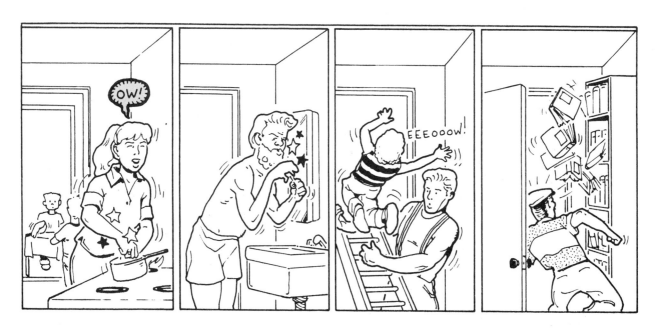

| We | were(n't) | eating breakfast | at 8:15. |
| He | was(n't) | sleeping | at that time. |

___ *A.   **Make sentences about the picture with these words and words of your own. (Say or write them.)**

EXAMPLES: At the time of the earthquake, some children were eating breakfast, and their mother was cooking. She wasn't paying attention.

At the time of the earthquake,

| A Some | man / men woman / women person / people child(ren) | | cooking. eating breakfast. doing exercises. paying attention. |
| He She They Someone Somebody | | was(n't) were(n't) | sleeping. shaving. leaving the apartment. drinking coffee and smoking. watching T.V. |

_____   _____ .

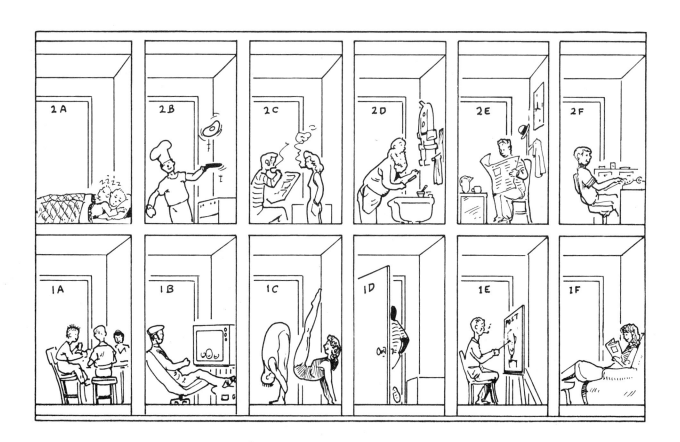

	Was	anybody	sleeping at the time of the fire?
What	were	you	doing then?
Who	was		helping?

B. Read the answers. Then finish the questions with these words.

EXAMPLE: 1. a: __Was__ anyone exercising at the time of the earthquake?
b: Yes, the people in Apartment 1C.

| Was | What | was | were | Who | Were | Where |

1. _____ anyone exercising at the time of the earthquake?

Yes, the people in Apartment 1C (were exercising).

2. _____ the people in 1A eating?

Yes, they were.

3. _____ _____ typing?

The man in 2F (was typing).

4. _____ _____ the children in 2A doing?

(They were) sleeping.

5. _____ _____ the man from Apartment 1D going at the time?

(He was going) to work.

*C. Make questions about the picture on page 149 with these words and words of your own. Answer them.

EXAMPLES: 1. a: Who was cooking at the time of the earthquake?
b: The man in Apartment 2B (was cooking).

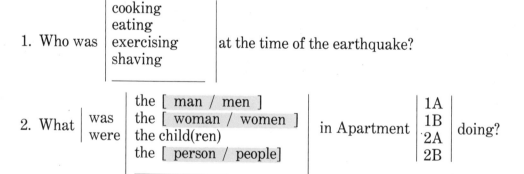

**D. Think about an emergency (an earthquake, a fire, etc.) or an important event in the past. Answer these questions: What were you doing at the time? What were the people around you doing? (You can work in small groups.)

PART FOUR / Quantity Expressions; Review

● Describing Amounts

	Plural		Noncount	
cigarettes	diseases	food	insurance
bicycles	checkups	sugar	medicine
doctors	medications	coffee	alcohol
bills	drugs	weight	exercise

	Less			More		
Plural	(not) any	a few	several	some	many	a lot of
Noncount	(not) any	a little	some	(not) much		a lot of

Use *any* and *much* only in questions and in sentences with *not*.
Examples: Are you losing any weight? I don't take any drugs.
Do you drink much alcohol? He isn't doing much exercise.

A. Choose the correct words.

My brother-in-law isn't living a very healthy life. He smokes [a lot of / ~~much~~]
                                                                      1.

cigarettes a day, and he has [a little / a few] drinks at every meal. He's taking
                                        2.

[several / a little] kinds of drugs, too. He's not doing [no / any] exercise, so he's
3.   **4.**

gaining [a lot of / much] weight. He goes on a diet every [few / some] months, but he
            5.   **6.**

doesn't lose [many / much] pounds. He has [many / much] health problems. He goes to
                    7.   **8.**

doctors only [a little / a few] times a year because he doesn't have [many / much]
                    9.   **10.**

health insurance. Of course he doesn't follow [any / no] advice.
                                                        11.

B.　Choose words and finish these sentences.

1. My | boyfriend / girlfriend / roommate | is(n't) living a healthy life because | he's / she's | eating / drinking / taking | a lot of / too much / too many | _____ .

2. I (don't) usually _____ | any / a little / a few / several / some / many / much / a lot of | _____ .

I	'm (not)	sitting	in the waiting room now.
The nurse	is(n't)	taking	the patient's pulse.
The patient	was(n't)	standing	in line an hour ago.
We	were(n't)	waiting	for the doctor at 2:00.

Wait, wait, wait! I began this appointment at 2:00 and . . .

Right now . . .

C. Make sentences about the picture story with these words and words of your own.

EXAMPLES: 1. At **2:00** I was **filling out forms in the waiting room.**

At _____ I was _____ ing _____

_____ .

10. At this moment I'm **standing here.**

At this moment I'm _____ .

Before
1. fill out forms
2. change clothes
3. weigh me
4. take my pulse
5. measure my blood pressure
6. wait for the doctor
7. listen to my heart
8. examine my eyes, ears, nose, and throat
9. wait in line for X-rays

At This Moment
10. stand here
11. wait for my prescription
12. lose a lot of time
13. feel impatient

	Are	you	checking	my heart now?
	Was	the nurse	examining	the records?
Why	isn't	he	taking	any X-rays?
What	was		happening	in the pharmacy?
Where	were	the patients	waiting	at 4:45?

D. Ask and answer questions about the picture story.

EXAMPLE: a: What was happening in the doctor's waiting room at 2:00?
b: A patient was filling out medical information forms.

*E. Choose words and finish these sentences. Answer the questions.

1. [Right now / At this moment] I'm _____ ing _____ .

   I'm not _____ ing _____ .

2. My [boyfriend / girlfriend / relatives / _____] [is / are] probably

   (not) _____ ing _____ .

3. [Tonight / Tomorrow / Next weekend / _____] [I'm / we're / _____]

   (not) _____ ing _____ .

4. At this time [yesterday / last week / last year / ____] [I / we / ____]

   [was / were (n't)] _____ ing _____ .

5. What [was / were] [you / your _____] doing at _____ ?

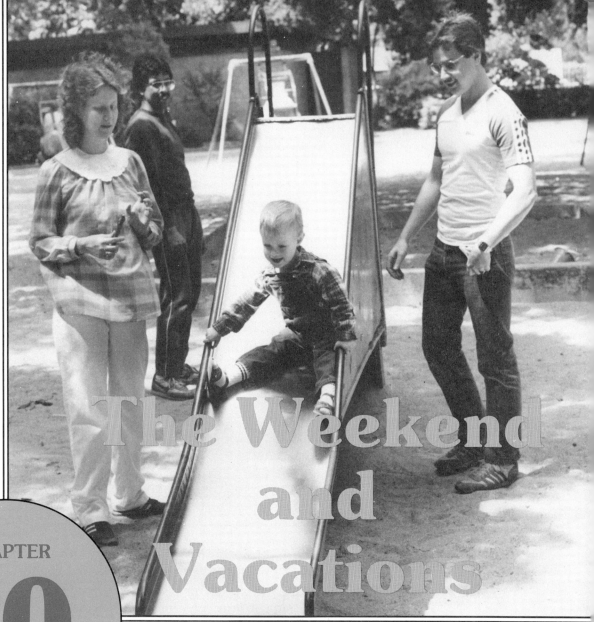

The Weekend and Vacations

COMPETENCIES:
Asking about and describing weather and distance
Making travel plans and telling reasons
Describing vacations

GRAMMAR:
Impersonal *it*
Review of verb tenses
Introduction to tag questions
Introduction to clauses

PART ONE   Impersonal *It*: Affirmative and Negative Statements

● Describing Weather and Distance

It's not going to be a good day.

Past	Present	Future
It was hot.	It's very cool now.	It's going to snow.
It wasn't raining.	It's not raining.	It won't rain.

A. Finish the sentences with these words and word parts. (Say or write them.)

EXAMPLE: 1. <u>It was</u> hot yesterday.

It	it	It's	it's	was	-ing

1. _____ _____ hot yesterday.

2. And _____ _____ sunny at noon.

3. _____ _____n't rain _____ at 3:00.

4. But _____ gett _____ cloudy.

5. _____ _____ cold last night.

6. _____ not warm today.

7. And _____ gett _____ cooler.

8. _____ cloudy now.

9. And _____ will get windy.

10. Maybe _____ going to rain.

Past	Future
It rained yesterday.	It may not get warmer.
It didn't clear up.	It might snow tonight.

B. Make sentences with these words.

EXAMPLE:
It didn't **snow** yesterday.
But it might **snow** today.

It didn't _____ yesterday.
But it might _____ today.

1. snow

2. rain

3. clear up

*4.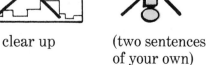
(two sentences of your own)

EXAMPLE: 5. It **was cloudy** yesterday.   It _____ yesterday.
               But it may not **be cloudy** today.   But it may not _____ today.

5.   6.   7.   *8.

be cloudy   be windy   get hot   (two sentences
                                                                       of your own)

It's one mile from here to the shopping center.

C. Make sentences about distances on the map.

EXAMPLES: **a:** It's two blocks from Tran's apartment to the bus stop.
                b: It's a half mile from the bus stop to the pizza place.

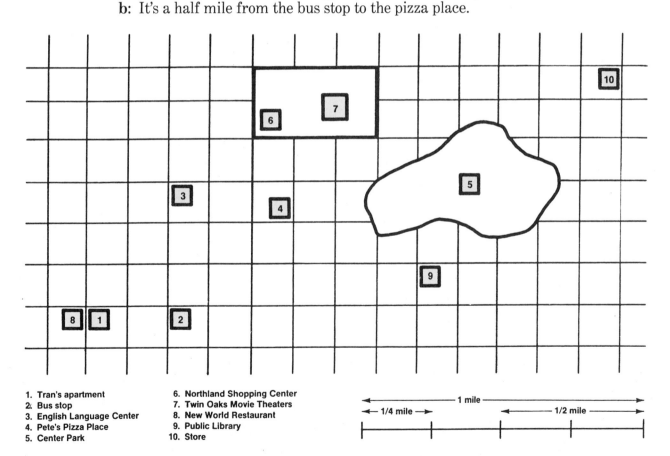

1. Tran's apartment	6. Northland Shopping Center
2. Bus stop	7. Twin Oaks Movie Theaters
3. English Language Center	8. New World Restaurant
4. Pete's Pizza Place	9. Public Library
5. Center Park	10. Store

**D. Look at a local map. Make sentences about the distances between places. (You can work in small groups.)

EXAMPLE: It's five blocks from school to the the bus station on Central Avenue.

_____ *E.   **Make sentences about the maps with these words and words of your own.**

It's about	1300 miles 700 miles	from	Miami New Orleans	to	New York. St. Louis.
	_____				_____ .

Yesterday it	was(n't) [hot / warm / _____] was(n't) [windy / cloudy / _____] was(n't) [raining / snowing] (didn't) [rain(ed) / snow(ed)] _____	in	Washington D.C. St. Louis. Toronto. Chicago. _____ .

Right now it's (not)	(getting) [hot / cold / _____] [raining / snowing / _____] _____	in	Detroit. Atlanta. _____ .

Tomorrow it	's (not) going to be [sunny / mild / _____] [will / may] (not) get [warmer / hot / _____] _____	in	Boston. Toronto. _____ .

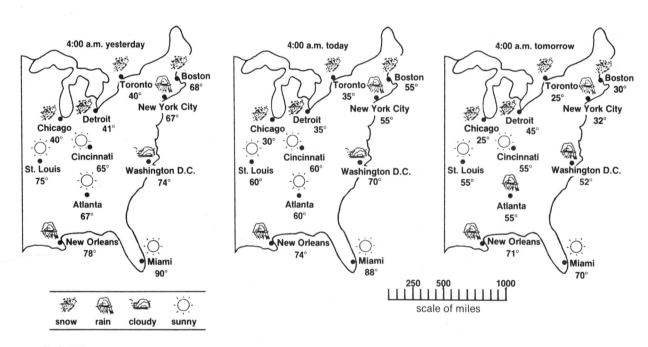

4:00 a.m. yesterday — Toronto 40°, Boston 68°, New York City 67°, Detroit 41°, Chicago 40°, Cincinnati 65°, St. Louis 75°, Washington D.C. 74°, Atlanta 67°, New Orleans 78°, Miami 90°

4:00 a.m. today — Toronto 35°, Boston 55°, New York City 55°, Detroit 35°, Chicago 30°, Cincinnati 60°, St. Louis 60°, Washington D.C. 70°, Atlanta 60°, New Orleans 74°, Miami 88°

4:00 a.m. tomorrow — Toronto 25°, Boston 30°, New York City 32°, Detroit 45°, Chicago 25°, Cincinnati 55°, St. Louis 55°, Washington D.C. 52°, Atlanta 55°, New Orleans 71°, Miami 70°

250 500 1000
scale of miles

snow   rain   cloudy   sunny

_____ **F.   **Look at a weather map in your local newspaper. Make sentences about it.**

EXAMPLES: a: At 6:00 this morning, it was very cold here, but it wasn't snowing.
             b: It's about 600 miles from here to Miami. It was much warmer there early this morning, and it was sunny.

PART TWO
Impersonal *It*: Questions; Introduction to Tag Questions

● Asking about Weather and Distance

It's a nice day today, isn't it?

a: Hi, Tran. Isn't it a nice day today?

b: No, it isn't. I got up early. I didn't have time for breakfast. I missed the bus. I ran to school for a test. And what day is it? Is it Monday, April fourteenth? No, it's not. It's Sunday, the thirteenth.

a: Of course it is. And it's a beautiful day, isn't it? What time is it now?

b: It's about 10:00.

a: Good. It's early. Listen, isn't there a place to have breakfast on the corner? Come on. Let's go together.

b: O.K.

a: And will you have time to go to the park after that? Do you want to have a picnic? It isn't too far to walk there, is it?

b: No, it's not.

a: And it might be fun to go to a movie in the afternoon. How far is it from the park to the theater in the shopping center?

b: Only a few blocks.

a: And then it will be time to have dinner, and then . . .

b: Great! Let's go. You know, it is a nice day today, isn't it?

	Is	it	far from here to the park?
	Is	it	going to rain?
How far	is	it	from here to the park?
What time	is	it	now?
What day	is	it?	

After a question with *not*, the listener usually expects a *yes* answer.

EXAMPLE: a: Isn't it a nice day?
            b: Yes, it is.

A. Ask questions for these answers. (Say or write them.)

EXAMPLE: 1. a: Isn't it a nice day today?
               b: Yes, it is. It's a beautiful day.

1. _____

   Yes, it is. It's a beautiful day.

2. _____

   No, it isn't. I don't think it's going to rain.

3. _____

   Yes, it is. It's very early.

4. _____

   No, it's not. It's not far from here to the movie theater.

5. _____

   How far? It's about a mile to the shopping center.

6. _____   _____

   The time? It's about 11:00.   The day? It's Sunday, April 13.

It's	far	to the store,	isn't it?	Yes, it is.
It's not	far	to the park,	is it?	No, it isn't.
It isn't	hot	today,	is it?	No, it's not.

We	can walk	to the park,	can't we?	Yes, we can.
We	can't walk	to the store,	can we?	No, we can't.

B. Finish the questions and answers with these words.

is	isn't	can	can't

1. It's a nice spring day, _isn't_ it?   Yes, it _____ .

2. It isn't going to rain, _____ it?   No, it _____ .

3. We can have coffee, _____ we?   Yes, we _____ .

4. You can't drive, _____ you?   No, I _____ .

is	isn't	can	can't	it	we

5. It's early, _____ _____ ?   Yes, _____ _____ .

6. It's not getting cooler, _____ _____ ?   No, _____ _____ .

7. We can walk to the park, _____ _____ ?   Yes, _____ _____ .

8. We can't walk to the movie, _____ _____ ?   No, we _____ .

*C. Choose words and use words of your own. Ask and answer questions.

EXAMPLE: **a:** What time is it now?
b: It's about 8:45.

What | time / day of the week / day of the month | is it [now / today] ?

It's (not) | [early / late / after 4:00 / _____] ,
[Tuesday / Thursday / Friday / _____] ,
the [twelfth / fifteenth / _____] ,
[windy / wet / cold / _____] out,
_____ , | is / isn't | it?

Was(n't) it [sunny / hot / cold / _____] yesterday?
Is(n't) it a [nice / beautiful / _____] day today?
Is(n't) it going to get [cool(er) / warm(er) / _____] tomorrow?

How far is it from your school to | your [house / apartment / _____] ?
the [park / _____] ?
a [coffee shop / _____] ?

PART THREE
Introduction to Clauses:
and, but, so, because, if

● Making Travel Plans ● Telling Reasons

Let's take a trip.

a: We're going to have a week for spring vacation, so let's take a trip.

b: Great idea! Let's fly to Florida. We can save money if we rent a beach apartment together.

c: Wait a minute. It's warm in Florida, but it might rain. If we travel to Arizona, we won't have to worry because it will be sunny every day. We'll stay at a hotel in the desert so we can relax by the pool.

d: I prefer the snow, so I'd like to go to the mountains. It might be fun to share a cabin.

e: I'd prefer to take a train through Canada because I want to see the scenery. We can stop in the big cities so we can go sightseeing, and we can have picnics at the lakes and go fishing, and we can go to festivals and fairs.

a: Very funny. Come on. Let's get the tents for camping. Where can we drive in about two hours?

> We'd like a nice hotel room, but we don't have much money.
> We can stay in tents, and camping might be fun.
> It's cold in the mountains, so we'll stay in a cabin.

A. Make sentences with these words. (Say or write them.)

EXAMPLES:

1. I love **the beach**,
     so I want to go to **Florida**.
   We can **drive** there,
     and then we'll stay **with friends**.
   It will be **fun**,
     but it won't be **expensive**.

I love _____ ,
  so I want to go to _____ .
We can _____ there,
  and then we'll stay _____ .
It will be _____ ,
  but it won't be _____ .

1.

the beach / Florida
drive / with friends
fun / expensive

2.

snow / Colorado
fly / in a cabin
cold / cloudy

3.

fishing / the lake
take a bus / in tents
sunny / hot

B. Finish the sentences with the words *and*, *but*, and *so*.

EXAMPLE:

1. We'd like to take a trip, **but** we don't have much vacation time.

We'd like to take a trip, _____ we don't have much vacation time. You can get
            1.

places quickly by plane, _____ plane travel is fun, _____ it's too expensive
            2.   **3.**

for us. Buses are uncomfortable, _____ we're not going to take one. Trains can be
            4.

very slow, _____ they aren't cheap. We want to go sightseeing, _____
      5.   **6.**

we're planning to see several cities, _____ we're going to drive.
            7.

| I like big cities | because | sightseeing is fun. = |
| Sightseeing is fun, | so | I like big cities. |

C. Finish the sentences with these words.

EXAMPLES:
1. We should go to the state fair **because** there will be a lot of interesting things there.
2. We'll want to see everything, **so** let's stay a few days.

| so | because |

1. We should go to the state fair _____ there will be a lot of

   interesting things there.

2. We'll want to see everything, _____ let's stay a few days.

3. We can share a room at a motel _____ it's not expensive.

4. It may be cool or warm, _____ let's take a lot of clothes.

5. We won't need to bring any food _____ they sell food there.

D. Make sentences with the same meanings.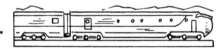

EXAMPLE:
1. a: We traveled by train **because** we wanted to see the scenery.
   b: We wanted to see the scenery, **so** we traveled by train.

We went to Canada last summer.

1. We traveled by train **because** we wanted to see the scenery. = _____

   _____

2. My family likes fishing and boating, **so** we visited some lakes. = _____

   _____

3. We stopped in a few cities **because** I love sightseeing. = _____

   _____

4. There was a music festival there, **so** we went to Vancouver. = _____

   _____

> Let's go to the festival   so we can hear music.

E. Make sentences with the same meanings.

EXAMPLE:
1. a: Let's stay at a campground **to save money**. =
   b: Let's stay at a campground **so we can save money**.

1. Let's stay at a campground **to save money**. = _____

   _____

2. We'll bring food **to cook**. = _____

3. We have to bring heavy jackets **to keep warm**. = _____

   _____

> You can use the pool   if   you stay at a hotel.
> If   you stay at a hotel,   you can use the pool.

F. Find the sentence parts. Then make two *if*-sentences with the same meanings.

EXAMPLE:
1. a: We can rent a beach apartment **if** we go to Florida. =
   b: **If** we go to Florida, we can rent a beach apartment.

1. We can rent a beach apartment   ____ we go to the mountains.

2. We'll stay in a cabin   ____ we spend time in Mexico.

3. We'll have to speak Spanish   _if_ we go to Florida.

4. ____ we take trains in Canada,   we can see beautiful scenery.

5. ____ we go camping,   we can get more information.

6. ____ we visit a library,   we'll sleep in tents.

_____ *G. **Choose words and finish these sentences. You can use the pictures for ideas, but add information of your own, too.**

1. On my next vacation, I want to go to [the beach / a big city / the mountains / _____] because _____ .

2. I love [the ocean / snow / the sun / _____] , so I'd like to _____
_____ .

3. If it's [sunny / hot / cool / wet / _____] at that time, we'll _____
_____ .

4. We can [fly / drive / take a train / _____] there, [and / but] then we might want to _____ .

5. I think we should [share a hotel room / stay in a cabin / bring tents / _____] so we can _____ .

   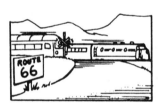

_____ **H. Tell or write about your last vacation trip or your plans for your next one. (You can work in small groups.)**

EXAMPLE: On my last vacation trip, I visited my relatives in San Diego, and I stayed at their place. We went sightseeing every day because they wanted to show me their city. We went to the zoo several times, but we didn't drive to the desert.

PART FOUR / *It* + Adjective/Noun + *to* Verb; Review

● Describing Vacations

Past	It was no fun	to take the bus.
Present	It's a good idea	to drive.
Future	It will be nice	to get home.

A. Make sentences with these words. (Say or write them.)

1. _____
   to get a hotel room / It / hard / was / .

2. _____ _____
   every day / rained / It / .   never sunny / was / It / .

3. _____
   It / all the time / no fun / to stay inside / was / .

4. _____
   to go there / wasn't / a good idea / It / .

5. _____ _____
   It's / to be home / good / .   to relax / will be nice / It / .

It was	too late	to take the bus.	(So I didn't take it.)
It's	too cold	to go out.	(So we won't go out.)

B. Make sentences with the same meanings.

EXAMPLE: 1. **a:** It was far, so we didn't walk to the beach. =
         b: It was too far to walk to the beach.

1. It was far, so we didn't walk to the beach. = _____

   _____

2. It was cold, so we didn't swim in the ocean. = _____

   _____

3. It was expensive, so we didn't eat in nice restaurants. = _____

   _____

4. Now it's late, so we can't take another trip. = _____

   _____

	It's	Saturday, April 12.	
	It wasn't	windy yesterday.	
	It isn't	raining now,	is it?
	It can	snow here,	can't it?
	It's	fun to travel,	isn't it?
	It won't	be too late to eat.	

	Is	it	going to rain tomorrow?
How far	is	it	from here to Canada?
What time	is	it	now in California?

We can get a room,	and	then we'll eat lunch.
It's hot in the desert,	but	it's dry.
I don't like buses,	so	I'm going to take my bicycle.
Let's stay home	so	we can save money.
I like to drive	because	it's comfortable.
We can go to a concert	if	there is one tonight.

_____ ***C.** **Make sentences, ask and answer questions, and have conversations about these travel plans.**

EXAMPLE: **a:** It's a good idea to travel to Vancouver because it's close to us, so it won't cost much to get there.
b: But isn't it cold there?
a: It's cold in the winter, but we want to take a trip in the summer.

TRAVEL PLAN
Vancouver, Canada

10 arrive at the bus station
11 check in at the hotel
12 have lunch at a restaurant
2 see the city by bicycle
4 go shopping
7 go to a concert

The weather in Vancouver in the summer is warm in the daytime. It doesn't get dark before 9:00 p.m., and then it gets cold very fast.

TRAVEL PLAN
San Diego, California

10 arrive at the train station
11 check in at the hotel
1 have lunch in the park
2 see the city by bus
5 go shopping
9 go to a show

The weather in San Diego in the summer is warm in the daytime. It doesn't rain. It gets cool at night.

Where should we go next year?

_____ ****D.** **Get travel brochures from a travel agency or information from a library. Make travel plans. Tell or write about them. (You can work in small groups.)**

APPENDIX

Irregular Verbs

Simple Form	Past Form	Simple Form	Past Form
be	was/were	meet	met
begin	began	pay	paid
bring	brought	put	put
buy	bought	read	read
choose	chose	ride	rode
come	came	run	ran
cost	cost	say	said
cut	cut	see	saw
do	did	sell	sold
draw	drew	send	sent
drink	drank	set	set
drive	drove	sew	sewed
eat	ate	show	showed
fall	fell	sit	sat
feel	felt	shrink	shrank
find	found	sleep	slept
fly	flew	speak	spoke
forget	forgot	spend	spent
get	got	stand	stood
give	gave	swim	swam
go	went	take	took
hang	hung	teach	taught
have	had	tell	told
hear	heard	think	thought
keep	kept	understand	understood
know	knew	wear	wore
leave	left	withdraw	withdrew
lose	lost	wrote	wrote
make	made	wring	wrung
mean	meant		